Also by Willard Spiegelman

If You See Something, Say Something: A Writer Looks at Art

Seven Pleasures: Essays on Ordinary Happiness

In the Frame: Women's Ekphrastic Poetry from Marianne Moore to Susan Wheeler (coeditor)

Imaginative Transcripts: Selected Literary Essays

Love, Amy: The Selected Letters of Amy Clampitt (editor)

How Poets See the World: The Art of Description in Contemporary Poetry

The Lives and Works of the English Romantic Poets

How to Read and Understand Poetry

Majestic Indolence: English Romantic Poetry and the Work of Art

The Didactic Muse: Scenes of Instruction in Contemporary American Poetry

Wordsworth's Heroes

SENIOR MOMENTS

SENIOR MOMENTS

Looking Back, Looking Ahead

WILLARD SPIEGELMAN

Farrar, Straus and Giroux ⬦ New York

Farrar, Straus and Giroux
18 West 18th Street, New York 10011

Library of Congress Cataloging-in-Publication Data
Names: Spiegelman, Willard, author.
Title: Senior moments : looking back, looking ahead / Willard Spiegelman.
Description: New York : Farrar, Straus and Giroux, 2016.
Identifiers: LCCN 2015048666 | ISBN 9780374261221 (hardback) |
    ISBN 9780374712990 (e-book)
Subjects: LCSH: Spiegelman, Willard. | Authors, American—20th century—
    Biography. | Authors, American—21st century—Biography. | College teachers—
    United States—Biography. | Aging—Psychological aspects. | Life change events—
    Psychological aspects. | Happiness. | Pleasure. | BISAC: SELF-HELP / Aging. |
    LITERARY COLLECTIONS / Essays. | SOCIAL SCIENCE / Gerontology.
Classification: LCC PS3619.P5432 Z46 2016 | DDC 814/.6—dc23
LC record available at http://lccn.loc.gov/2015048666

Designed by Abby Kagan

www.fsgbooks.com
www.twitter.com/fsgbooks • www.facebook.com/fsgbooks

10 9 8 7 6 5 4 3 2 1

To the memory of Peggy Amsterdam, Michael Harris,
Carolyn Horchow, and everyone else who left
the party much too soon;

and for Ken, from start to finish

We think the purpose of a child is to grow up, because it does grow up. But its purpose is to play, to enjoy itself, to be a child. If we merely look at the end of the process, the purpose of life is death.

—ALEXANDER HERZEN

Prepare for death. But how can you prepare
For death? Suppose it isn't an exam,
But more like the Tavern Scene in Henry IV,
Or that other big drunk, the Symposium?

Remember, everybody will be there,
Sooner or later at first, then all at once.

—HOWARD NEMEROV, "SPECULATION"

... all human beings are divided
into those who wish to move forward
and those who wish to go back.

—LOUISE GLÜCK, "FAITHFUL AND VIRTUOUS NIGHT"

CONTENTS

PREFACE

First comes the acknowledgment, then the preparation.

We all know what our end will be, but few of us can predict when we will meet it, or when it will surprise us. Or how. We come into the world alone—with a mother there, of course, and in most cases some attendants—and we leave it alone, often with different attendants to bear witness.

And the preparation? I place myself in the skeptical camp of the wry, witty, sage Howard Nemerov: "How can you prepare for death?" The Renaissance offered lessons in the art of dying well, on the theory that another, eternal world awaited. A secular man who believes in life's finitude, a world that comes to an end when he does, gains little hope from the consolations of traditional religion. Life has not been a dress rehearsal. It is what we have, and all that we will have had.

If I can pin wishful hopes on a metaphor for something beyond, I shall stay with Nemerov: What could be better than the raucous company of Shakespeare's Falstaff, that exuberant, bloated,

Rabelaisian figure of excess and wisdom? Perhaps the more high-minded tipsiness of Plato's *Symposium*, with Socrates as the presiding deity of rational hedonism. A heaven consisting of intelligent discourse among friends who share food and drink, conversation, teasing, warmth, flirting, and laughter: I can imagine none better. To a nonreligious nonbeliever like me, any image of an orthodox afterlife, one based on rewards and punishments, seems implausible. I'll give my vote instead to Charles Lamb, who asked, "Sun, and sky, and breeze, and solitary walks, and summer holidays, and the greenness of fields, and the delicious juices of meats and fishes, and society, and the cheerful glass, and candlelight, and fireside conversations, and innocent vanities and jests, and *irony itself*—do these things go out with life?" Alas, they probably do, although the temptation to believe otherwise is strong. Lamb's contemporary John Keats had an even more benevolent, generous view. To his friend Benjamin Bailey, he mentioned one of his favorite speculations: "that we shall enjoy ourselves hereafter by having what we called happiness on earth repeated in a finer tone and so repeated." Like Nemerov and Keats, we can merely speculate; we never know.

I also find it difficult to know how to label the following pages. Some years ago, I wrote a book called *Seven Pleasures: Essays on Ordinary Happiness.* I learned from friends across the country that the personnel in some bookstores, not quite knowing how to classify it, had placed it on the "Self-Help" shelves. At first the news troubled me. I felt I had been misunderstood and undervalued. Those clueless clerks had ignored my true literary value. Then I took a more sanguine view. If my writing could help some readers, I thought, I would have provided a noble service. And if putting my book in a place where it might actually sell, rather than leaving it to sit on the shelf forbiddingly called "Essays," then so much the better.

The following pages are essays. They are also a memoir, in the form of backward and forward glances by a senior citizen who has reached his biblical allotment of threescore years and ten and who anticipates more years of pleasure, if luck and health hold out. They glance at paths I have followed and others I have not taken.

And they acknowledge the fact that, as the literary critic William Empson observed, even a life rich in intimacy retains an essential isolation. I have a partner of many years' standing. I have friends. I have family. I have had a career. I think hard about two lines from one of Wordsworth's early poems: "And many love me, but by none / Am I enough beloved." Does Wordsworth's speaker, Matthew the schoolmaster, mean that no single person has given him the special all-consuming, all-nurturing love he needs? Perhaps. A still more powerful, cogent understanding of the lines would have it that all the love in the world will not make up for our abiding, primitive solitude. We come into the world alone, with a cry. We exit alone, to confront the final eternal silence. The fun, all the pleasure and adventure, lies in between.

SENIOR MOMENTS

TALK ✍

t began, like so much else, with my mother. One of her quick and piercing put-downs of a person—usually a woman—of whom she disapproved was "She's got a mouth on her, that one."

My mother had a mouth on her. She was hardly the only one with such a mouth, on either side of a large extended family, but hers was the first voice I heard, the one that summoned me and then my younger brothers to strict obedience, sent us fleeing or cowering from her irritation or disapproval, and set us on the edge of embarrassment when it expressed clear, usually negative assessments of, and verdicts about, other people in public places. My mother had strong opinions and was never timid about sharing them, at times inopportunely. Annoyance was her basic humor. It was not until I was twenty-five or so that I learned that "aggravation," like "nauseous" and "anxious" (I'll include "gorgeous" just to add a positive note), was not a Yiddish word, but rather, ordinary English. "If I didn't play golf," she once said, "what would I do for aggravation?"

My mother had no internal censor. To think before she spoke never occurred to her. Whatever went through her mind came out of her mouth. She was not a nonstop talker, a babbler, a nervous monologuist; instead, her speech had an explosive force. You never knew what might provoke one of her stealth attacks. She favored two modes: the command and the surprising judgment. Examples of the former: "Billy, sit up straight"; "Richie, you look awful: get a haircut." Many mothers traditionally think of themselves as helpful domestic disciplinarians. Commands come naturally from them, like sunshine or rain.

My mother's opinions were more unanticipated than her orders, in part because she issued these obiter dicta as definitive pronouncements. On Shakespeare: "He's much too talky." About the French horn: "It's not a solo instrument." She was sensitive to the visual arts as well. Of her first trip to Italy: "Everything is old and broken and dirty, but the table settings were impeccable." She made her trek through the museums and galleries: "If I had to see one more Madonna and Child, I thought I would plotz." Encountering the Ghiberti *Gates of Paradise* at the Baptistery in Florence: "If the Church just sold those doors, they could solve world hunger."

Neighbors and relatives inspired ethical and practical as well as aesthetic judgments. Of an uncle who had dropped us from his will: "The weasel should rot in hell." About a social-climbing woman who lived around the corner and who always thought herself better than her neighbors and her surroundings: "The next time I see her, I won't know who she is before she doesn't know who I am." In her youth, my mother looked like Vivien Leigh, a diminutive dark-haired beauty. Petiteness meant a lot to her; size offended her, as did facial hair on men and showy makeup on women. No makeup was almost as bad as too much. Excess weight she considered close to a sin for both genders. To a niece, home from college: "You're getting fat." To my brother, either before or after serving him a piece of chocolate cake: "You're getting too fat." This was an all-purpose accusatory observation disguised as aesthetic-moral diagnosis. She had her fixations. We could never figure out their cause, but they had a kind of eternal permanence in her life. Like many obsessions, they deepened and hardened as she aged. And she never relented in her efforts to articulate them.

To my longtime boyfriend, whom she had not seen in several years, in a hotel lobby before a family dinner: "Ooh! What happened to you?" (His hair had turned gray.) She never hesitated to remind us that our hair was too long, our clothes inappropriate, our posture too slouchy. If she had ever had a daughter, one of them would have long ago killed the other. Sons were in some ways a disappointment to her but also a considerable relief.

A steward of domestic order, she never stinted with her helpful household hints: "If you keep your kitchen drawers closed, crumbs won't fall in," or "Eat over the sink so I won't have to sweep the floor." Crumbs had no chance in our house. Neither had insects. She did not take kindly to animals. "I don't need a dog," she said. "I have three children." Her aversion to all nonhuman creatures, great and small, was so strong that my mother took what seemed to be considerable, even manic pleasure in drowning ants in our driveway with boiling water. When asked whether she thought they might attack us indoors, she said, "You can never be too careful." Had she known any Jains, she would have felt no sympathy for, no understanding of, their belief in the sanctity of all life. And she certainly would not have been able to hide her disdain.

Unlike Shakespeare's Cordelia, whose voice was "ever soft, / Gentle, and low, an excellent thing in woman," my mother's was loud, grating, often shrill, and always capable of penetrating the bowels of any department store when she was trying to locate a wayward child. She uttered suggestions and requests in the same tone as reprimands and commands. When I hear a Philadelphia accent, I hear her. She recognized no difference between the Normandy invasion and a trip to the supermarket. She handled everything

with peremptory force and at top volume. Going out for our painful weekly Sunday dinner, she more than suggested: "Drink a glass
of milk now so we won't have to buy one for you at the restaurant."
Waking up my youngest brother, home from college for spring
vacation, one Saturday morning at eight: "You can stay in bed, but
I need those sheets *now*." When I once suggested that she seemed to
harbor some anger—always directed outward to the world but
with no discernible cause—she barked, "I'm entitled to my feelings." Self-reflection never led to moments of hesitation, if only
because self-reflection did not have a place in her ways of dealing
with the world. Neither did silence. For my mother, a room without a radio or a television turned on was a room that lacked vitality.
Noise and life were synonymous.

Before her memorial service, the presiding rabbi went on a fact-
finding mission with her sons. "Would you say that your mother
had a pleasing, quiet manner?" he asked. I knew I had the opening
line for my remarks to friends and family at the funeral chapel.
I repeated his question; the audience roared. I struck exactly the
right tone; I knew I had said the right thing.

My mother often did not say the right thing. At least her sons
thought so. But at the same time, she was never manipulative or
guilt inducing. She meant well. Although her openness with
strangers—she always talked, to everyone, everywhere, in restaurants and supermarkets—was well intended, it struck her sons as
embarrassingly aggressive, even threatening. She performed an
early version of what we now call networking. No one was safe. Once
we all were lined up at a restaurant. My mother could never stand
patiently in silence. She began chatting up the people in front of us.
"You're from Cleveland? I have cousins in Cleveland." My brothers
and I were rolling our eyes, hoping that perhaps the ground would
open up. The family in front not only knew her Ohio first cousins;
they lived next door to them. She made the world a smaller place.
She always connected with fewer than six degrees of separation.

Conversation—an exchange of ideas and opinions with something like forward motion—did not figure in her repertoire. I had to learn from others how to perform conversational give-and-take. But when I think of how I turned instinctively away from my mother's habits and mannerisms, I have to acknowledge, reluctantly and late, that I also inherited many of them. All children, especially in adolescence, find their parents embarrassing. Most of us outgrow the itchy need to disown these creatures from another planet as we start making our own mistakes and recognizing that we have inherited more than our looks from Mom and Dad. We have become them. We are from the same planet. I always sit up straight. I consider a well-made bed a symbol of both domestic and inner discipline. Nothing, neither fever nor backache, has ever prevented me from making my bed thirty minutes after I have left it. Often when I am alone, I eat over the kitchen sink. The crumbs go right down the drain. I, too, have a mouth on me. Sometimes I speak too quickly, unthinkingly, or sharply. I often talk to strangers, in line or at parties, and establish social contacts. And when I do, I can hear Edith, my mother. After all, we call our native language the mother tongue. I accept the resemblance and I move on.

It was not only my mother who got me talking. It was an entire extended family. I can't remember anyone who was silent, with the exception of my paternal grandfather, an innately soft-spoken, modest man with a commanding wife who ran his life. Several small strokes had deepened his natural reticence by the time I came on the scene. Some of my relatives talked with greater speed and volume than others. I was the only child around. I imitated my elders. I walked, and I talked in sentences, before my first birthday. Enthusiastic and hyperactive, rather than precocious, I listened, and then I imitated. My large family made its impression on me through language. We had no athletes; no one who earned a living by physical labor; no workers, mechanics, or outdoorsmen. A day on the golf course was about as rough-and-tumble as it got. The men were all businessmen and salesmen, of varying degrees of success, or doctors, lawyers, engineers, and scientists. The women did not work outside the house. They were mothers and homebodies, with the exception of my great-aunt Annie, who, widowed young, ran the cigar stand at her Atlantic City residential hotel. She knew tobacco; she also knew which of her gentlemen customers, some of whom became gentlemen callers, preferred which kind of whiskey. The very fact that she worked made her exotic to her great-nephews.

Many of my other relatives had names that now seem caught in amber. Names, like all kinds of fashion, go in and out of style. They change. You might have thought that many American Jews born between 1900 and 1940 belonged—if you saw their first names in print—in a manor house. Their names, but not their voices, were quasi-English. Few of them actually cut a figure from a 1930s black-and-white comedy of manners, whether English or American, when they spoke. They might have dressed like William Powell and Myrna Loy in *The Thin Man*, but their voices, their accents, told a different story. The men did not sound like Leslie Howard and Cary Grant, nor the women like Katharine Hepburn, Gladys Cooper, or Billie Burke. Where are those names now: Alfred, Bernice, Clifford, Edith, Evelyn, Gladys, Hortense, Maxwell, Mildred, Myra and Myron, Norma and Norman, Sylvia and Sylvan? They were never plucked from the Old Testament.

All of my great-aunts and great-uncles were but one generation removed from the shtetls of Eastern Europe. Their parents had made the voyage out; my grandparents and their siblings became Americans. The habits and customs of the Old World, all the stuff of family legend, inflected with an American effort to "make it new," filtered into my consciousness like Ovidian myths or Kipling's *Just So Stories*. Whatever differences separated them, these people were all talkers. Some had accents as memorable as the cigars the men smoked and the perfumes and dusting powders the women wore. My grandmother's older brother Manny married a woman from Boston whom everyone considered hoity-toity. To me, they were both colorful rare birds. They lived in Greenwich Village, where Manny, who sported a beret, played chess in Washington Square Park on Sunday afternoons. Aunt Gert wore her white hair in a chignon and accessorized with long dangling earrings. Uncle Manny ran a suspenders factory, which switched to belts just in the nick of time, but regardless of their status as manufacturing tradespeople, he and Gert qualified as my family's sophisticated bohemians, a delectable hybrid, both familiar and exotic. They encouraged in me hope for the possibility of escape.

Few of the Philadelphia relatives were like this. Several, like my father's mysteriously named uncle Foots-and-a-Half, and my mother's first cousins Will and Grace (Grace was Aunt Annie's elder daughter), had shady, Runyonesque connections. Reckless danger, or even misdemeanors, had no part in my immediate family, so these outliers cut a peculiarly enticing figure. Modest bootlegging, usually around Passover, was said to have occurred during the 1920s, well before my time. Prohibition did not stop domestic routine. The family justified home brew on the theory that bathtub wine was at least kosher even if bathtub gin was probably not.

We also had gamblers on the periphery of the family, skeptically admired but also held at arm's length by their more bourgeois siblings and cousins. In an age when, out of courtesy, we called all familiar adults "Aunt" and "Uncle" whether they were related or not, Uncle Will and Aunt Grace stood out. They moved around, a lot, not by their own choice. Will and Grace left Philadelphia under a cloud and resettled in Miami Beach in the early 1950s, there to open a bridge and poker club and escort the local widows on gambling cruises to Havana and St. Thomas. The sound of Grace's manicured fingers on the ivory mahjong tiles at poolside ("Three bam!" "Four crack!" delivered in her whiskey baritone voice) possessed an inexplicable sonic splendor, still memorable decades later.

Grace, always smoking her unfiltered Camels, spent an hour a day putting on her makeup. She lasted well into her nineties, still wobbling on her high heels to make an entrance at the country club or even the delicatessen. A couple of more distant louche relatives, equally sketchy, played the numbers in Atlantic City. Some got run in for tax evasion. Every family needs a handful of dubious characters to add some romance to suburban reality.

Even more than names, bodies, and smells, I remember sounds. I remember language. Everyone talked about everything—except their inner lives, that is. The family directed all talk outward, to and about the world. Like all lucky children, I must have heard the same family tales and legends—no one really knew or cared if they were true—countless times. "Tell me again," I remember asking my grandmother, "about how your father hid the five younger sisters in the back room after the family scandal." The scandal: Lena, the second daughter, married before Rae, the eldest. Only when Uncle Sam, fresh off the boat, took Rae for his wife did the family feel unashamed enough to let the other girls out into the light. Eudora Welty reminisced about sitting under the piano in Mississippi, listening to the grown-ups talk. She attributed her own storytelling successes to early story listening. I can still hear, through the years, my family chattering: assertively, ironically, simultaneously. Language was the best way to make one's mark. I hardly knew it at the time, but language became my life's leitmotif.

Call it phonophilia: love of sounds, at least certain ones. Phonophobia is its opposite. Whenever I read or hear accounts of life in the traditional WASP, Scandinavian, Calvinist, or similarly repressed household, a family with silence as well as secrets, I sigh with wonder and some envy. All families have secrets, some well hidden, but not all maintain silence as the default mode with regard to everything. There was no silence in my house, or locked doors for that matter, nor was there any in the homes of my grandparents, with whom we bunked—my father, mother, and I—before we got a house of our own. My father had left the army in 1946, when I was less than two years old. For the next two years, we divided our time between his parents' light-filled house near the northern end of Philadelphia's Broad Street and my mother's widowed mother's gloomy tenth-story apartment some blocks away. Whatever temperamental and social differences between the two sides of the family, one thing remained constant: Silence was suspect. It went with sleep.

My father's sister, a young naval bride in 1944, wrote to her parents about the eye- and ear-opening events at a Sunday dinner at the Officers' Club on the base where she and her husband were stationed. My uncle, a tall, handsome lieutenant, sat at one end of the table, to the right of the admiral's wife. My aunt sat at the other end, to the right of the admiral himself, who must have been delighted with this leggy, blond, talented, and vivacious Veronica Lake look-alike. Liveried military servants ladled out the soup, then served salad, then the traditional roasted haunch of animal accompanied by the overcooked vegetables that decades later Julia Child taught Americans to forgo. Sherry preceded the meal, and strawberry shortcake followed it. The servants poured coffee from a silver service. Then the gentlemen retired to one room, the ladies to another.

My aunt had only recently escaped from Philadelphia. What most impressed her about the event was not the food. She reported her amazement to her parents: "We had Sunday dinner at the Admiral's table. Only one person spoke at a time." She had left behind not only bagels and lox but also high-pitched, raucous Jewish excitement. At home, the men and women might have engaged in separate conversations, but they never occupied different rooms before or after dinner. The family had, for starters, fewer rooms. Compared with what Aunt Wilma knew from home, this dinner with the officers was like *Babette's Feast*, the 1987 movie based on Isak Dinesen's story about the collision of repression and exuberance, self-denial and hedonistic delight.

No one in our family had ever heard, or even imagined, such a thing: "Only one person spoke at a time?" Doesn't nature abhor a vacuum? The only way that one person alone would be speaking would be if everyone else—against all mathematical probability—had a mouth full of food. At home, the custom of the single speaker never took hold. "Politesse" did not come easily.

Does simultaneous, as opposed to consecutive, speech indicate vulgarity or exuberance? Despair or joie de vivre? A lack of attention or an excess of it? Unresponsiveness to others or heightened concern? If you interrupt someone mid-sentence, do you force him to raise the volume and the speed of his delivery? Neurologists who have tested the brain waves of people listening to music, in concert halls or at home, conclude that it is not the music itself but the pauses within the music that prime the brain for further activity. The silence, not the sound, constitutes the real neurological event. In conversation without pause, there is no event. The conversation becomes a nonstop easy-listening station: all babble, all the time.

In families like mine it was easy to confuse nervous anxiety with genial enthusiasm. Sometimes it was hard to tell one from the other. A raised voice could mean affirmation, love, enthusiastic greeting, or just as likely a warning about tripping and breaking your neck. If danger lurks constantly—where you go, or with whom, what you eat, what you wear, what the weather looks like—then prescriptions and proscriptions have to be delivered in stentorian tones. Hollering signaled love. "Watch out, or you might die" was the essential message. This style of vocalizing had charm when you saw it represented in movies or television. I think of Gertrude Berg's alter ego, the affable Yiddish yenta Molly Goldberg, who "yoo-hoo'ed" her way across the tenement air shaft from her window to her neighbor's. In reality, it made my ears tremble and my flesh creep.

Rodgers and Hart's "Manhattan," a nostalgic lullaby to old New York, describes the clamor of peddlers on the Lower East Side as "sweet pushcarts gently gliding by." We glamorize the past, smoothing over its difficulties, making the noxious delectable. The desperate need of rag merchants, clothing salesmen, knife grinders, and fruit vendors to eke out a living becomes the stuff of melodious sentimentality.

Spoken language, even more than writing, brings us together and sometimes pulls us apart. The majority of all the people who have ever lived have been illiterate. But barring physiological or psychological infirmity, or elected vows of silence, everyone has talked. And talk means more than necessary communication, expressions of needs and desires, affirmations and denials, commands and compliance. I'll go so far as to deem conversation the essential human art. Even the origin of the word signifies its status as a marker of civilized life: from Latin, via medieval French, an act of living or keeping company, of turning about with other people. The "con" prefix joins us together; the "verse" signifies our turnings. Recently, standard black English has created a contemporary linguistic back-formation—a verb from a noun from a verb—to "conversate," suggesting a more engaged, active form of communication. I imagine that conversating qualifies as a more animated form of conversing.

Language came early to me. First words, then sentences. I was like a pony out of the starting gate. As a firstborn, prodded by and responsive to the attention of an extended family, I performed with ease. I knew polysyllabic words from an early age. A now ninety-year-old relative (another "aunt") has reminded me that when I was three, I looked at my six-month-old second cousin and called her a "Technicolor baby." I had just seen my first Walt Disney cartoons.

I came upon the dictionary and the almanac at the same time. I memorized words and facts with equal greed. Exposure to the wittily packed librettos of Gilbert and Sullivan operettas came shortly afterward. "I answer hard acrostics, I've a pretty taste for paradox, / I quote in elegiacs all the crimes of Heliogabalus": The Major General's patter song from *The Pirates of Penzance* won me over at the age of nine both by its jaunty melody and, even more, by those mouth-filling words. I had as little an idea of acrostics and elegiacs as I did of Heliogabalus, but I made it my business to find out who and what they were.

Not knowing the meanings of certain words, names, or sounds has almost as much power as learning them, of mastering a language. Curiosity impels us. Such arcane researches had no practical or even social benefit, but they gave pleasure, not just the pleasure of showing off by performing, but something deeper, a combination of the physical and the imaginative. I learned that words have sound and meaning. Although I didn't know this at the time, I was also discovering the essential charms of poetry itself, with its combination of the semantic and the non-semantic. Rhythm, rhyme, and music: melody enhances the meanings of words and the power of communication.

How do we converse, or conversate, with one another? Like clothing and names, speech is style. Cultures as well as individuals have different standards of talking, making sense, going back and forth. Conversation, too, is a kind of performance, subtler and not hewing to a script. And it has a history. It has changed over time and in different places. It may be intimate—between lovers or close acquaintances—or it may be something more public. Here are some adjectives that do not apply to the best conversation: "one-sided," "monopolizing," "condescending," "preachy," "abrasive," "hectoring," "loud," and "rude." However many people it involves, conversation is, like chamber music, an exercise in intimacy, of give-and-take, of what Plato, who recorded the talk of one of history's first and finest talkers, called "dialectic," a word etymologically related to "dialogue." Conversation moves forward, or back and forth in starts and stops, like drama itself. That philosophy, democracy, and drama all began in fifth-century Athens says a great deal about the far from incidental relations among them.

Many of the great talkers—Oscar Wilde and Samuel Johnson at their most clever—would not qualify as masters of conversation. They were performers, delivering bons mots, aphorisms, put-downs, and clever witticisms de haut en bas. The person who excels in conversation has mastered the art of listening as well as speaking. Monologuists and epigram makers belong to a different species. Speechifiers are linguistic bullies. Talkers, on the other hand, relish the game itself. Someone serves, and another person responds. The volleys can engage more than a pair of participants. Pronouncements tend to put an end to conversation rather than enliven it.

One can trace the outlines of the history of conversation from Plato's *Symposium*, the original feast of drinking, talking, philosophizing, and flirting, to Trimalchio's stupendous banquet in Petronius's *Satyricon*, then through the salon culture of prerevolutionary France and the coffeehouse culture of eighteenth-century England, to the late-night talk show apparatus of American television, and from there to Internet chat rooms, where virtual people have replaced live ones and where cloaked anonymity often substitutes for honest openness. Animals communicate with one another for practical purposes—mating, protection, aggression—but only human beings talk for the sheer pleasure of it.

Stephen Miller's 2006 *Conversation: A History of a Declining Art* takes an amiable stroll through "talk" from ancient Greece to the present American moment. Miller sounds like a modern Jeremiah, lamenting the fact that the latest technology—beginning with television and moving through the newest avatars of computer devices—has severely undone the conditions of, and the prospects for, "civilized" discourse. Like any person given to nostalgia, Miller looks back to golden ages of conversation, to Enlightenment France and Britain above all, and finds in today's world an absence of the charms that permeated earlier cultures. Such regret is probably misplaced. Not only have witty banter, sharp riposte, and cordial disagreement always been in short supply, but everyone with an ounce of politeness, tolerance, and fellow feeling can attest to conversations he has had that have challenged, amused, and satisfied him in equal measure. Everyone has known great and amusing talkers even if everyone is not a great talker himself. Listening makes its own demands and has its own satisfactions.

Henry Fielding called conversation "this great business of our lives." I would go further: conversation is the cornerstone of democracy and of commerce. We conduct business through conversation. I have been assured by friends who have international dealings that the Japanese and other Asian peoples are adjusting slowly to, or even resisting, a culture in which Skype and other kinds of teleconferencing have come to replace face-to-face personal interchanges. Traditionally, in a one-hour business meeting in Japan, the first fifty-nine minutes consist of pleasantries and cordial compliments, and the actual sealing of the deal occurs only at the end. Can we dispense with the niceties and cut to the chase? Apparently not: you need those first fifty-nine minutes to ensure the last one.

We conduct business through talk, but we also derive infinite impractical pleasure from chatting. It binds us to one another. Not the screaming we see on television, nor the banal bantering with stars and starlets we see daily—and nightly—but the ordinary give-and-take we have with neighbors; friends and relatives; strangers encountered on airplanes, on trains, and in bars and pubs; and, through the miracle of serendipity, people we run into on the street. Good humor and surprise, the willingness to be pleased or to change one's mind about matters large and small, signify a cheerful, sanguine disposition. Flexibility of temperament, combined with the ability to listen as well as to speak one's mind, without harassing one's mates, ensures civil decency. It's not only good fences but also good talking that makes good neighbors.

Dancing, that most useless of human activities, teaches both grace and manners. People of a certain age were trained in the drill of the ballroom. It is everyone's obligation to invite everyone else to the floor. "May I have this dance?" begins the game, and the gentleman leads the lady (in the new age, gender reversal is legitimate) for a four-minute excursion, after which he says "Thank you" and escorts her back. Conversation will perform much the same function, helping us with grace and manners, but only if mutual respect matches the courtesy of the back-and-forth ritual. Growing up, we were told that politeness forbids a frank discussion of certain topics—money, politics, religion, and sex, above all—but those are the topics most people want to talk about. They are certainly the ones that everyone has knowledge or at least opinions about. When Lytton Strachey uttered the word "Semen?"—as question or challenge—to Vanessa Bell after he had noticed a stain on her dress, her sister, Virginia Woolf, said, "We burst out laughing. With that one word all barriers of reticence and reserve went down. A flood of the sacred fluid seemed to overwhelm us." Bloomsbury conversation had entered a new era. The modern age had begun. Camp came out of the closet. More than a century later, sex is no longer hors de combat at the dinner table, or anywhere.

Other prohibitions remain. At some genteel men's clubs in London, New York, and wherever Anglophilia retains its grip, certain quaint customs and modest restrictions still prevail. I have witnessed them. One does not conduct business of any sort at lunch. Even waiting for your host at table, you are not permitted to take out a pen and begin writing. Writing is work. Reading is permitted, but note taking, like using a cell phone, is forbidden. And if you are a club member who arrives for lunch unaccompanied, you sit at the "long table" with other solo members, some of whom you may know but others not. Introductions are frowned upon. You are men of the world and are expected to keep up your end of a conversation without injecting unnecessary trivial personal information, like your name. And you don't ask questions; no "Who are you?" and "Where are you from?" and "What do you do?" Better to begin with the weather and proceed to the news, always mindful not to trample on your neighbors and their points of view. In some cultures—traditional Japan comes again to mind—the very asking of a question is considered the height of rudeness. One works through indirection, teasing out someone's preferences and responses, rather than asking for them directly, succinctly.

Keeping matters light can also keep them trivial and mindless. Good talk maintains a rhythm, like a piece of music, a ground between highs and lows, the serious and the amusing, the philosophical and the personal. A thread must weave itself logically through the conversation with the appearance of natural inevitability. And there must also be surprises, turnings away, changes of pace and tone that enliven and lead unpredictably to new matters.

At a smart dinner party in Dallas some years ago, a group of ten took to a tastefully appointed table. As servers came in with a first course, our hostess disapprovingly announced, "Oh, I told Susie I wanted the green china, not the red, this evening." Without missing a beat, I observed unpremeditatedly, "Those people in Bosnia don't know the meaning of hardship." The hostess blushed and then laughed. Disaster averted, the meal proceeded smoothly. The red china disturbed neither the soup nor our enjoyment of it. All of us could tell the difference between real trouble and what we might call First World problems. Laughter punctuates the best conversations, always. Social communication thrives on unexpected improvisation.

A laissez-faire approach to talk—allowing it to flow aimlessly but seamlessly—has much to recommend it. Like a stream of consciousness, the stream of talk goes in its own unpredictable way. An alternative conversational gambit looks more like state planning.

Dr. Oliver Wendell Holmes, the so-called autocrat of the breakfast table, was not the only convener or autocratic choreographer of talk. Some hosts or, more likely, hostesses enjoy orchestrating a conversation. Many times I have sat in numbed attendance waiting my turn to be called on by Monsieur or Madame Professor Host or Hostess. This is the Dinner Party as Command Performance. One doyenne of Dallas society calls this Jeffersonian conversation in honor of the master of Monticello, and she insists upon a single conversation, which means that the table, regardless of the number of participants, has become a graduate seminar, with the hostess making inquiries of everyone on whatever subject she has deemed worthy of attention. This modern version of a Socratic dialogue (along the lines of peremptorily declaring "Let's talk about beauty"; "What is the ideal city?"; or "What defines a good life?") has much to recommend it, at least in theory. In practice, the frequent slowness of response, not to mention the potential awkwardness of the diners' opinions, makes for the conversational equivalent of pulling teeth. As does the fact that people speak in turn, with no volleying between them. What we get instead is a series of little monologues, not a Socratic dialectic—thesis-antithesis-synthesis—with its constantly refining, contradicting, revising, slow unsteady movement. Sit-and-deliver performances tend to sobriety rather than sparkle. One welcomes modest fireworks at the dinner table.

The hostess's seminar plan inhibits spontaneity. It serves, indeed guarantees, a forced equality. Everyone, moving clockwise or counterclockwise, has his or her say. Planning the conversation is the equivalent of arranging the place cards. One wants to leave nothing to chance, so one scripts the talk. I'll take my stand with Joseph Mitchell, who was a great writer in part because he was a great listener. He said, "The best talk is artless, the talk of people trying to reassure or comfort themselves." Elizabeth Bishop, riding on a bus from Nova Scotia to Boston (in her poem "The Moose"), overhears something similar, "an old conversation / —not concerning us, / but recognizable, somewhere." Revelations, wisdom, and courtesies come about at least as much by accident as by deliberation.

Natural, active, engaging talkers sometimes bridle or even freeze up when required to perform. And every table needs at least one good listener; not everyone needs to talk to ensure the steady flow. Talkers play to both their sparring partners and their silent admirers. Is there a perfect number for dinner conversation? Experience suggests six to eight. With that number, you can indeed have a single conversation without military rigor or without the enforced etiquette of old-fashioned dinner parties at which the hostess begins by turning to the guest of honor on her right and speaks to him while the host, at the distant other end of the rectangle, turns to the leading lady at his right and does the same. Everyone follows suit. As if by clockwork, the perfect hostess knows to adjust her tempo and turns to the gentleman at her left for the next course. Counterclockwise and then clockwise: it seldom works with symmetrical results, but you get the idea. By this model, dinner conversation is more like a dance, a pas de deux, than an honors seminar. But it is work, not play.

Food and drink are helpful, if not always required, to loosen tongues. Whether in the aristocratic salons of Paris or the coffeehouses of eighteenth-century London, the bar on television's *Cheers*, where everyone knows your name, or the late-night drink in a hotel where you chat with the guy on the adjacent stool and reveal truths to someone you will never see again precisely because you will never see him again, civilized consumption and civilized conversation are mates. The mouth is an erotic organ. We use our mouths for lovemaking, but that is private activity. Talking and eating are equally oral but social too. Food is a stimulant, and wine a lubricant, to conversation. Candlelight creates a more than visible glow. It enlightens and enlivens the talkers.

Above all, difference, or what goes by the name "diversity" today, counts for a lot. Birds of a feather may flock or eat together, but only polite disagreement, moderate dissension, can make for conversation. Someone old, someone young, someone exotic, someone refined, someone naive: the blend can vary, but it is necessary. W. H. Auden dedicated his poem "Tonight at Seven-Thirty" to M.F.K. Fisher. He prefers a table of six, with no doting lovers, no children, and no malcontents on hand. A god of any sort would be inappropriate, because he'd probably bore everyone. A genius or a prima donna might overwhelm everyone. (I once had dinner with a great man of music, at a table for six. There was only one topic of conversation, and it was not merely music itself.) Auden asks for

> one raconteur, one gnostic with amazing shop,
> both in a talkative mood but knowing when to stop.

My own preference would include tablemates of different ages and backgrounds. Even more, I want a table where the subjects of conversation will include language itself, where different tongues can speak on behalf of different cultures as well as sensibilities, and where linguistic cognates and differences give rise to wonder and laughter. At a country dinner party, my longtime partner and I were seated among six older, richer WASPs, who had all the worldly experience, manners, money, and breeding of their class. The conversation turned to idioms from one language that are virtually untranslatable into others. The hostess gave an example from Hungarian. That set the bar very high for the rest of us. Someone else, who had worked for the Foreign Service, offered an example of something in Arabic. I tried, with less panache, to work with the concision of Latin's ablative absolute, which requires longer English phrases to reproduce. Other people contributed examples from garden-variety Spanish and French. And so it went, until (my) Ken played the trump card. In Yiddish.

"My grandfather used to say, in moments of annoyance, to my grandmother, 'Minnie, don't hock me a chinick.'" The other guests leaned in, eager for enlightenment. Ken explained patiently. "A 'chinick' is a teapot; 'hock' is to chop." Someone, although no one at this party, might have recognized a cognate in "gehochte leber," "chopped liver." "Don't chop, bang, or knock me a teapot" means "Get off my case; leave me alone."

One lock-jawed, well-traveled preppy lady of a certain age said through her gleaming teeth, "Oh, I like that one." And she turned to her husband of many decades and said gleefully, "Louie, don't hock me a chinick." I doubt that the formulaic phrase entered their subsequent tête-à-têtes.

I have long since forgotten what we ate at that meal. I do remember what we said. Some people have the capacity to remember what they put into their mouths. I work the other way. I remember what I have uttered and what I have heard.

Language, it has often been said, is the most astonishing creation of humankind. We must have invented it at the same time we invented God. Language allows us communication with those we confront. Having a deity encourages us to address someone we can never see or know but only talk to. He does not reply, for the most part, which is just as well. Job, hearing God speaking from the whirlwind, does not actually have a conversation with him. And Job's earlier conversation with his three comforters, sadists all, provided him with little solace. Face-to-face talk is still, for the most part, preferable to the telephonic variety. "What are you wearing?" begins Nicholson Baker's short novel *Vox*, about phone sex. Like phone sex, talking on the phone is not as good as the real thing, but it has its place. Can we like the online voice better than the one attached to a person we can see at the same time? I cast my vote for the fuller engagement, person to person and in three dimensions.

Conversational tics such as stuttering and interrupting that do not offend or irritate us in person may seem exaggerated and more offensive when you cannot see the person with whom you are talking.

A phone conversation resonates differently from a live chat. Looking and seeing complement listening, hearing, and speaking. This psychological or neurological difference has made for changes in socializing. One young friend recently told me that he and his contemporaries, making dates via the Internet, tend to observe one strict rule: no phone conversations before a face-to-face meeting. Text first, talk later. And I often wonder whether the better way to enjoy opera is at a live performance, where you get to see action, drama, sets, and costumes, as well as hear the music, or on the radio, stereo, or computer stream, where you get only the voices and are not distracted by your eyes. In the first option, you have the total experience, but in the second you have the undistilled, pure pleasure of sound. You can hear better when you are only listening.

In "Losing Track of Language," one of her great poems of travel, Amy Clampitt tackles the issue of conversations with strangers in public places, but with a twist: the languages are foreign. For someone like Clampitt or me, getting something wrong in a foreign tongue can be as much fun as getting it right. Linguistic competence and the pleasure of chance encounters work together. Her poem recounts a train trip between the South of France and Italy. Clampitt and her companion "sit wedged among strangers" in a train compartment. As the landscape changes, "words fall away, we trade instead in flirting / and cigarettes; we're all rapport with strangers." She thinks of Petrarch, that earlier pilgrim in the Vaucluse, who perfected the sonnet and immortalized his beloved Laura therein.

Their Italian compartment mate hears "Petrarch" and responds enthusiastically:

> A splutter of pleasure at hearing the name
> is all he needs, and he's off
> like a racehorse at the Palio—plunging

> unbridled into recited cadenzas, three-beat
> lines interleaving a liquid pentameter.
> What are words?

Words are, of course, all that we have of Petrarch, of Laura, of all the dead: "Whatever is left of her is language," says the poet, before restarting in a different key:

> —*E conosce* (I ask it to keep the torrent
> of words from ending, to keep anything
> from ending, ever) *anche Sapphò?* Yes,
> he knows, he will oblige. The limpid pentameter
> gives way to something harsher: diphthongs
> condense, take on an edge of bronze. Though
> I don't understand a word, what are words?

But of course she understands. She intuits the tone beneath the words, the meanings within the ancient Greek that she knows only through translations of Sappho's fragments. Landscape and language both fall away, but the poet has made contact, via her two dimly understood foreign tongues, with this stranger on the train. Loss has been her subject, but gain has been her accomplishment.

The poem ends as it began:

> The train leaps toward Italy; words fall away
> through the dark into the dark bedroom
> of everything left behind, the unendingness
> of things lost track of—of who, of where—
> where I'm losing track of language.

Amy Clampitt, by her own admission, was a "garrulous creature." She loved language; she loved long, mouth-filling words. She wrote poems that often send a curious reader to the dictionary. She was aware that everything fades and disappears but also that the hold of language, however tenuous, is the strongest thing that binds us together.

Any language lover knows the comedy of miscommunication when trying to master a foreign tongue. And also the thrill of improvised successes. Many years ago, at a beach in the Algarve, I— in my pathetic attempt to weave something like Portuguese out of strands of French and Spanish—charmed a couple of Portuguese boys by explaining to them W. C. Fields's reason for preferring gin to water and for abjuring the latter. "Non bevo acqua," I said, "perchè in acqua pesce fucka-fucka." Nothing was lost in translation. The young men knew just what the great comedian meant. And we ordered more *vinho verde*.

And years later, at a large dockside restaurant in Genoa, where one sat at large tables with strangers dining on the fruits of the Ligurian Sea, we began chatting with two young Italian sailors, who by this point were rollicking with high spirits and a lot of wine. "Siete marinati?" I asked, noticing their sailors' uniforms. They guffawed. "Certo!" My mistake: "sailors" is *marinai. Marinati* means "marinated," "pickled," "dead drunk." And those *marinai* were *ben marinati*.

And once, on an Italian train, squeezed like Clampitt into a small compartment with five other travelers, I used literature—as the poet herself did—as a way of opening up a brief conversation. Auden might have been right: six is the perfect number for talking at table. In the hot car chugging from Florence to Parma, I sat between an older Chinese couple, clearly Italian residents, on one side, and, on the other, a well-coiffed lady of a certain age who spent the trip on her cell phone talking to her daughter in Rome. Across from her sat a middle-aged priest who was deeply immersed in the sports pages of Milan's *Corriere della Sera*. Across from me, an Italian university student dozed a bit. I had taken for my leisure reading Giuseppe Tomasi di Lampedusa's *The Leopard*. Published in 1958, this great elegiac novel reads like something from the previous century. Luchino Visconti's sumptuous film starring Burt Lancaster, Alain Delon, and Claudia Cardinale only increased the glow of the book itself. I looked up and saw that the girl across from me had awakened and was also reading: *Il gattopardo*. I interrupted her and said, "Noi leggiamo lo stesso libro!" This alerted the Chinese couple, the glamorous signora, and even the priest. Everyone had memories of reading it at school. They all loved it. Auden was wrong when he said that "poetry makes nothing happen." In our case, a shared literary experience caused a momentary coming together of people who would never see one another again.

Some things go without saying, or without the need of a known language. I can never forget the annual Christmas visits of the woman whose daughter married my brother-in-law. Carina, an exotic French-Algerian model, the kind of woman who literally turned men's heads when she walked down the street, had taken up with Philip, a savvy, handsome New York rogue. Their daughter arrived shortly afterward, a little early. At that point, Rose, the French grandmother, began her pilgrimages to visit the blessed child. At Christmas in the West End Avenue apartment of my in-laws, Grand-mère Rose and Nanny Evelyn, her American counterpart, spent the holiday week cooking, decorating a tree, and billing and cooing over the child. From infancy through adulthood, Yasmine had the total attention of the grandmothers. The rest of us were superfluous. Rose spoke no English. Evelyn had no French. They understood each other perfectly. They spoke the international language called Grandmother. This language consists of exclamations, verbs of admiration and exaltation, and adjectives in the superlative. No translation was necessary.

Emerson said, "No man should travel until he has learned the language of the country he visits. Otherwise he voluntarily makes himself a great baby—so helpless & so ridiculous." I have always prided myself on attempting rudimentary remarks in the language of any country I visit. In Japan (see pages 63–66), becoming a great baby gave me pleasure as well as stimulation. But wanting to learn language—any language, indeed every language—must have had its origin in those first babblings from my mouth and the mouths of my extended family. I moved quickly from talking to reading to writing, from language in the air, and the ear and mouth, to language on the page. I stayed in school because I was good at school. I learned foreign languages. Had I been born later, I would have taken advantage of semesters abroad and the chance to perfect my speaking of those languages. I have had to satisfy myself with schoolboy forays into semi-competent French, Italian, and German. I became a university professor of English.

And then, for an unplanned, entirely unexpected learning experience, I moved to Texas, where both language and everything else seemed, initially, foreign.

DALLAS

One always begins to forgive a place as soon as it's left behind.
—DICKENS, *Little Dorrit*

ere is a formula for staying young well beyond the days of youth: Grow old in a place where you do not think you belong. You will feel like an adolescent, because adolescents always consider themselves outsiders. Then, after decades, just as you have gradually habituated yourself to your surroundings, pack up and leave. It is time for another, perhaps the final, beginning.

On a broiling, torpid, sweat-inducing day (there is no other kind in north Texas from June through September) in August 1971, I alighted at Love Field, the in-town airport that served Dallas before the completion, three years later, of the Dallas/Fort Worth International Airport. DFW, celebrated for being larger than the island of Manhattan, was appropriately Texas-size. But in 1971, I was twenty-six years old, timid, and not sure I was ready for the big Wild West. Luckily for me, a smaller airport made for an easier, warmer welcome.

I had never ventured farther south than Mount Vernon, Virginia, or farther west than Chicago except for a job interview in Dallas seven months earlier. Western Europe I knew. The western United States, real America, I knew not. I found my way to a car rental agency. While filling out the necessary papers and providing credit card information, I chatted with the woman behind the desk. Her hair, piled high, was shellacked, helmeted, and of a shade of blond never seen in nature. Her nails could have cut through wire. She had more color on her face than a rainbow. And her alarmingly perfect teeth—well before the age of ubiquitous dental cosmetology—glistened like pearls.

Henry Higgins could do justice to regional Texas dialects, but I cannot. Besides, they have now largely gone the way of most other local accents, owing to migration patterns and the homogeneous speech of television newscasters. I retain a fondness for those voices that exist mostly in my memory. No orthography can capture this woman's pronunciation. Every syllable contained a diphthong of practically infinite, honeyed duration, and there was not a pure vowel to be heard. "How yew?" she asked.

"I'm fine," I replied. "How are you?"

"Ahm doin' good, mahty fahn. Whatcha cummin' down heah to doo?" she politely inquired.

"I'm going to be an assistant professor at SMU," I said, still wet behind the ears and already beginning to get plenty wet all the way through, in spite of the air-conditioning.

"Whah, that's so nahs. What'll yew be teachin'?"

"I'll be in the English department."

"Yew've cum down heah to teach us English? Whah, yew don't even talk lahk us!"

Even today, more than four decades and two Bush presidencies later, the Lone Star State seems more exotic and alien to many Yankees than Nepal or Bora-Bora. And I certainly know people who have traveled around the world but not across the Red River.

Remember: Texas was an independent republic for an entire decade, from 1836 to 1845. And if some of its citizens get their way, it may yet again secede from the Union. As a longtime resident, I always assure my skeptical friends and relatives that they are both correct (it is strange) and wrong. As with speech, so with other customs and habits: America, like the rest of the world, has become smaller, and most places mirror one another. Anyone whose image of Dallas and Texas comes from the Bushes and Rick Perry, or from television's J. R. Ewing and his large, dysfunctional family, all of them living in a single house at Southfork despite their wealth, will be disappointed, or perhaps relieved, by the reality. Ditto anyone who has seen Robert Altman's *Dr. T and the Women*, in which I know that I saw more fancy society women wearing hats (hats!) in the first thirty minutes than I have in more than forty years in this city.

Although it occurred to me on that August morning long ago to rush back to the tarmac to see whether I could reboard the plane for its return flight to Boston, I gamely stuck it out. I acclimated myself, in many ways, to life in Texas, if never as a Texan.

When I finally arrived at my tiny apartment near the university, the temperature outside was 104 degrees; the air-conditioning inside was set at 68 degrees. Six days later, my rented car having been returned and my determination to live as a pedestrian ("It's a city ... Who needs a car?" I asked myself) having got the better of me, I decided to take the bus to the suburban branch of Neiman Marcus.

Before my arrival, I knew exactly three facts about Dallas. The first, of course, was that President Kennedy had been shot there almost eight years before. The place, to a northerner's eyes, was a bastion of reaction, a spawning ground for hatred, America's city of shame. Like everyone else of my generation, I had spent the weekend of November 22 to 25, 1963, glued to a black-and-white television set. Second, I knew that Greer Garson, that noble Mrs. Miniver and a feisty Elizabeth Bennet to Laurence Olivier's Mr. Darcy, had settled down there with an oilman. She lived in the same glamorous high-rise apartment building, a rarity in a city of single-family houses, as the soprano Lily Pons.

And I understood that Neiman Marcus was the mother church in a city that took both religion and commerce very seriously. Some years later, an older woman of my acquaintance took great comfort in the final stages of dementia from the knowledge that she would be buried right across from the same Neiman Marcus store that was my destination. She had lost almost everything else from her life, including the details of her own identity, but she remembered shopping at Neiman's. She remembered glamour.

My landlord pointed me in the direction of the bus stop, two short blocks away. I walked there at 9:30. He had neglected or forgotten to mention that buses ran infrequently on weekends. At 10:30, the mercury already at 97 degrees and still rising, the bus arrived to take me less than two miles to the stylish shopping mall. Having spent an hour in the heat, and another in the super-cold indoor environment, I—nothing daunted—decided to walk home. The next day, I came down with laryngitis and a fever.

One adjusts to climate after a while, or tries or pretends to. In Dallas, one estivates, staying under cover as much as possible from May until the third week of September, when, always on schedule at the equinox, a norther comes through and breaks the back of summer. People in the North suffer from one kind of seasonal affective disorder. Too little light produces too little serotonin. Vitamins and artificial illumination may alleviate the condition. Summer in the South comes with its own seasonal disorders: fatigue and irritability are the principal effects. For much of the year, the sun becomes an enemy; one is grateful for window shades and sunscreen. Bright light oppresses; it neither animates nor inspires. The old song "Home on the Range" has it right: the skies are not cloudy all day. Day after day. I have never found a cloudless day something to hope for. Someone who reads from afar the newspaper weather report learns that in Dallas the high one day in July is 99 degrees, and the low is 75. What he does not learn is that the low temperature is struck for about ninety seconds right before sunup; by 9:00 a.m., the mercury has resettled comfortably into the high eighties, and it doesn't begin to drop until well after midnight. When I moved to Dallas, everyone assured me that we had "dry heat." That might have been true a century ago, but Dallas is not Phoenix, Albuquerque, or El Paso. Over the decades, not only has the air become more humid, as a result of population growth and the attendant vegetation, lawn watering, backyard swimming pools, and other man-made bodies of water; it has also become more unbreathable. Industrial pollutants, sometimes blown north from Mexico, sometimes of more local origin, can hang over the city like a miasma for days, even weeks, at a time.

Scientists now have data on those of us who might say, along with T. S. Eliot's speaker in *The Waste Land*, "Winter kept us warm." These include people who fear the sun, who quickly develop skin cancers, whose bodies adjust badly to humidity, who perspire easily, who become resentful, cranky, and hard to live with in the heat. Summer depression strikes fewer people than the winter variety, but it exists. I read a study that said that in India the incidence of depression is higher in summer than what passes for winter; in Italy, it's the opposite. Who knows why? One thing is certain: at home in the States, or anywhere else, you can always add layers of clothing to keep you warm, but there are limits to what you can remove.

The postwar growth of the American South owes everything to the development of universal central air-conditioning as well as to low state taxes. For the first half of the twentieth century, Dallas was still, like Houston and Atlanta, a relatively small town. The women and children of the bourgeoisie went away in the summer to the mountains of Colorado and New Mexico or to the lakes of the upper Midwest. Menfolk worked in their offices, ate in restaurants, had mistresses. Life in Manhattan and Philadelphia was much the same. Families were sent to beaches on the Jersey Shore or Long Island, where the men came, by train, for weekends. In Dallas, you had to travel farther to get away from the heat. Fewer people could afford to make a short break. Trains were inconvenient. Anyone who stayed in Dallas slept outdoors on screened-in porches, with electric fans to move the hot air around. People took cold baths. Women wore light clothing; no one exercised or expended calories unnecessarily. Frequent hydration helped to restore depleted energy. And everyone got used to the situation; no one knew anything different.

I sometimes think of Wallace Stevens, who went west of the Mississippi only once in his life, and of how he, like Elizabeth Bishop, divided his imaginative energies between the North of Connecticut (Nova Scotia for her) and the South of Florida and Cuba (Brazil, as well as Florida, for her). Like any New Englander sensitive to the awakening of spring, he understood the gradual opening of the soil, atmosphere, and human spirit as a simultaneous revival of erotic energies. And he knew how to take the measure of his region through nuances of color and temperature: "The man who loves New England and particularly the spare region of Connecticut loves it precisely because of the spare colors, the thin lights, the delicacy and slightness of the beauty of the place. The dry grass on the thin surfaces would soon change to a lime-like green and later to an emerald brilliant in a sunlight never too full. When the spring was at its height we should have a water-color not an oil and we should all feel that we had had a hand in the painting of it, if only in choosing to live there where it existed" ("Connecticut Composed").

What Stevens called the "mythology" of his region—composed in equal parts of topography and weather, as well as history and human culture—has its Texas equivalent. A New Englander gains hope in the spring. After winter's dulling and dimming, lengthening daylight and warmer temperatures cause the human sap, like that of the trees, to rise. In the South, the process works the other way around. Life begins in autumn, a special bonus for an academic like me who customarily thinks in terms of the school year. As the days shorten, as first the nights and then the days themselves begin to cool, the human spirit emerges from hiding. We start to breathe, and to think, again, following summer's oppressive languor. For much of the year, the sun is too bright, the colors too vulgar. In October, the harshness relents and nature restores a measure of softness to itself and to us. We come back to Stevens's "water-color" from the garish "oil" of summer, when there was no place to hide from the sun. Dallas in July and August is a de Chirico picture: bright, geometric, and seemingly devoid of human life. The landscape becomes entirely metaphysical. When summer's emptiness at last gives way to the paradoxical fullness of a mild winter, we regain a central human outlook. Between November and April, any day in Dallas might have a freeze or a modest snowfall. One year, I celebrated Thanksgiving here in shorts and T-shirt; the next in sweater, corduroys, and boots to protect against icy streets. One year, we can pretend we are back north with the Pilgrims; the next, we are likely to be in Palm Beach. At least we no longer feel like outcasts in the baked land of relentless summer.

Weather is one thing; topography and landscape make for a different but related story. It is normal to feel a preference for native soil, so transplanted New Englanders often have difficulty in most of Texas, which has two seasons: summer, and everything else. North Texas is prairie—neither desert like El Paso, nor hilly like Austin, nor semitropical like Houston. God almost certainly never intended for anything to grow here except live oak, hackberry, mesquite, bois d'arc (pronounced "bow dark," and so called, according to myth, because Noah used this hardwood to build his flood-withstanding boat); some sad-looking bushes like the ligustrum, the boldly shaded crape myrtle, the salmon-colored quince, the Carolina jasmine, the trumpet vine (all healthy and easy transplants); and the hardy redbud, a cross between tree and bush, of no particular attractiveness in shape or foliage except for two weeks in early spring, the end of February, the beginning of March, when it opens its luscious, plum-colored blossoms. I had never noticed this tree in the Northeast, although it grows there, probably because it is only one among many providers of spring color. In Dallas, it stands more or less alone. Erotically beautiful and, like most erotic phenomena, painfully ephemeral, the redbud might symbolize the way beauty breaks in everywhere, even when and where we least expect it. Most trees here are small by the standards of Colorado or Connecticut. In some neighborhoods, you used to pay a fine if you sawed down mature plantings. A Yankee will always miss lilacs and horsechestnut trees, poplars and ginkgoes, but in Dallas we do have the lovely, delicately aromatic wisteria and the catalpa, whose popcornlike blooms brighten the streets at least two months before their northern cousins open up.

A half century ago, you could still find some cotton and alfalfa fields within the present city limits. Dallas's soil is clay, inhospitable to agriculture and to construction as well. Every building foundation that has not gone down to bedrock—that is, every residential property in the region—moves with the seasons, in soil dry and cracking in the summer, wet and spongy in the winter. To minimize the shifting of the foundations, especially during arid spells, homeowners used to be instructed to soak the perimeters of their houses. During a decade of unhappy home ownership, I went outside every morning in July, hosing down my 1927 house, which stood on an old-fashioned pier-and-beam foundation. So did my neighbors. We watered our houses.

Dallas was for most of the past century the country's largest city not located on navigable water. Its very reason for existence has never been ascertained. John Neely Bryan, the city's so-called founding father—its first Anglo resident—pitched a cabin here in 1841. He died in 1877 at the State Lunatic Asylum, to which he had bus, said that "Dallas itself is a monument to seeing who can put up a glassier, tonier-colored, mirror-plated skyscraper; not much class at all that I could see," although she allowed that in the adjacent countryside, where her cousins lived, "it's another matter." The motel where Bishop stayed looks out over an expressway that is really Dallas's Main Street, a thoroughfare that moves the populace along a north-south axis. Traffic, not water, flows in Dallas. To a poet whose life and work were nurtured by the comfort of a location— Key West, Brazil, Nova Scotia, and, in the last chapter, the Boston harbor—a landscape with no water in sight offered neither beauty nor inspiration. In Bishop's eyes, nature had either been suppressed by the human quest for urban life or never been present. In either case, it was indiscernible. She sent me a polite thank-you note after her return to Boston. In it, she said that she and her friends traveled into the piney woods of east Texas after visiting Dallas, "where we saw the saddest little towns I have ever seen. We saw a road marker that said 'Poetry—Three Miles.' If poetry is in as feeble a condition as 'Poetry,' I don't think there's much hope for it in Texas."

In certain sectors of the ever-expanding and ever-contracting "metroplex"—what we call Dallas and Forth Worth, forty miles apart but growing into each other like a molecular coupling—large commercial buildings of no particular style seem to have been dropped by helicopter into the soil. That's how the landscape struck the late Ada Louise Huxtable, doyenne of American architecture critics, when she visited in the mid-1980s. A man-made lake occupies a big space near downtown Dallas; its waters are mostly still and muddy, its surrounding vegetation brown scrub. But it offers shade and respite. The downtown, until recently a nine-to-five hive for worker bees, has come back to life modestly as a result of close-in housing, the conversion of department stores and banks into condos and apartments, and an imposed "arts district," which the city fathers wisely realized would help tourism and commerce. It boasts buildings by the Pritzker Prize–winning architects Norman

Foster, Philip Johnson, Rem Koolhaas, Thom Mayne, I. M. Pei, and Renzo Piano, plus a majestic bridge over the Trinity River by Santiago Calatrava. The masterful Piano pavilion for the Nasher Sculpture Center (2003) has been embroiled for years in a kind of real estate controversy not unique to Dallas: an adjacent condominium tower, sheathed in fiercely reflective glass, casts shadows into the museum and is ruining, according to museum officials, the gorgeous outside sculpture garden. The battle has taken on David-and-Goliath proportions.

An arts "district" Dallas may possess, but a district is not the same as a neighborhood. It is imposed rather than organic, dictated and not natural. The automobile still rules here, as in most of the United States. Few people walk, except for the earnest, mostly middle-aged women, doing their cardiovascular best. In the days before these sturdy and determined exercisers, if someone was seen on the streets in certain posh suburban neighborhoods, he would be stopped by the police, politely questioned, and then, especially if he was a person of color, driven to his destination. The efforts to produce a mass transit system have attracted a matched set of commuters: workers from the predominantly affluent white suburbs heading south into town in the morning, and African-American and Hispanic workers, often domestic ones, heading north. Both groups reverse directions for the evening commute.

The city has begun to encourage high-density living. It calls it the new urbanism. It wants to allow people to live close to where they work. But walking is still a dicey proposition. The sidewalks do not cooperate. They tend to be crooked, narrow, uneven, and cracked; they often have utility poles or trees growing in the middle; they do not allow two people to walk abreast, let alone groups of people walking in opposite directions. And we have one even more challenging obstruction: the heat. In April and October, you would probably break a modest sweat during the afternoon. In May and September, you certainly would; from June to August, you'd be as wet and baked as I was when I walked home from my first foray to the suburban Neiman Marcus.

Dallas is not handsome. Not even its most ardent boosters, were they honest, would claim beauty for it. It has lovely houses, charming blocks, some almost accidentally organic neighborhoods, and some random, spectacular residential and commercial buildings. Like most American cities that came of age after the automobile took over our lives and our landscape, it falls into the same category as Gertrude Stein's native Oakland: outside downtown, there is no *there* here. The city just goes on and on, one giant suburb. One neighborhood looks much the same as the others.

But if you live long enough in a place, you become sensitive to subtleties of climate and landscape. Even Bishop allowed that a former schoolmate whom she visited lived in a part of town that "was certainly pleasanter than the rest of it." Some backyard gardeners of my acquaintance have performed miracles, creating urban oases of Zen-like calm or perfecting the Roman ideal of *rus in urbe*, making a plot of urban ground into a miniaturized countryside. As the poet Gerard Manley Hopkins observed in a letter, "What you look hard at seems to look hard at you." Tiny perceptual calibrations and readjustments change your self-awareness as well as your sensitivity to your surroundings. A single tree can redeem a vast flatness; a single cloud can temper an oppressive summer day. Small gifts are small mercies, like Lady Bird Johnson's wildflowers that carpet the interstate highways in March and April.

One's definitions of well-being, happiness, comfort, and gratitude undergo subtle changes. Spring rains, especially when accompanied by pyrotechnic lighting effects, elicit the sweet odors of new beginnings, and even the random terrifying tornado can lift the spirit if you see it from afar. The occasional ice storm or snowstorm not only brings the city to a halt but also performs fleeting wonders on foliage and roof eaves before disappearing like a dream within two days. Bereft of New England's autumnal palette (we have no maple trees here, and the live oak is an evergreen that drops and replaces its brown-green leaves slowly during a four-month period), one notices more delicate coloration. We have the nandina, native to Japan, spreading its delicate fanlike leaf clusters and its red berries, which complement those of the pyracantha all winter long.

I once asked a newly arrived colleague whether she missed the change of seasons in upstate New York, and she said, "You forget, Willard, that I'm from New Mexico, and I regard green as an unnatural color." The deserts and mountains around Albuquerque and Santa Fe demand a visual readjustment so that one can register the rainbow that moves from palest yellow to deepest brown. In Dallas, the challenge is tougher still, because urban growth has inevitably denatured much of the terrain. Still, nothing proves more strongly the truth of the old adage that everything is relative than an exchange I had in my first year with a student who asked me the same question I asked my junior colleague: "How did it feel to move here?" I told her I'd never seen any place as flat and brown as Dallas. She replied, "Well, I'm from Lubbock, and I have never seen any place so rolling and green." I visited Lubbock many years later. She had it right.

The "Big D" immortalized by a great toe-tapping number in Frank Loesser's 1956 *The Most Happy Fella* was the city two characters had fled from in order to find happiness in Napa Valley. Dallas is not—or has not been until quite recently—a tourist destination. People come here on business, for conventions, to visit friends and family, and sometimes just to change planes. I doubt that anyone has logged on to a travel website and said to a spouse or partner, "Hey, dear, let's spend a week in Dallas, see the sights, hit the shops, do the town." You can't really *do* Dallas, in the way you can explore Paris or Kyoto. People my age will remember a certain promiscuous Debbie, who did "do" Dallas, at least in a pornographic film. Things change, however. With three major museums in Fort Worth and the more-than-respectable ones in Dallas, north Texas has be-gun to attract art lovers who have a long weekend to spare. If you build it, they will come, not too many and not for too long, but we are now on the map.

Even the most refined aesthete, however, cannot spend an entire life in a museum. He must move out into the world. Fortunately, for aesthetes and everyone else, you can move here and you can live here. Population has increased exponentially. Corporations like American Airlines, J. C. Penney, and Exxon relocated their head-quarters to north Texas within the past four decades, to take advan-tage of low taxes and cheap land. Finding an older native in Dallas is as difficult as finding a decent bagel. Seventh- or eighth-generation Dallasites, rare as hen's teeth, are self-proclaimed royalty. But Dallas worships money more than lineage, just as business always trumps history in matters like the architectural preservation of neighbor-hoods. "Make It New" might be Dallas's motto. It's the American way. Block after block of Victorian domestic architecture and many early Frank Lloyd Wright–inspired prairie houses have long since been demolished. Virtually anything from before 1960 qualifies for inclusion in a "historic district." Neighborly rival Fort Worth has profited from its second-city, poorer-cousin status and has man-aged with an infusion of capital from the billionaire Bass family to redeem a redbrick late-nineteenth-century downtown neighbor-hood called Sundance Square, slightly Disneyfied but pleasant and pedestrian-friendly.

What Dallas lacks in charm and soul it compensates for in ameni-ties. It is the land of shopping, indeed of the shopping center—the upscale mixed-use factory outlet, and other centers of all sorts. Did Robert Frost say, "Something there is that doesn't love a mall"? He hadn't visited Dallas. A recent student of mine, from a French family transplanted to Dallas, has an older sister who did her college major in something called luxury management. She is returning to Dallas from Paris this year: there is more luxury for her to manage here.

Across the street from the golf course at the ritzy Dallas Country Club stands Highland Park Village, a congeries of faux-Spanish buildings housing an ever-changing cast of haute couture boutiques (on my most recent visit: Jimmy Choo, Harry Winston, Saint Laurent, Christian Louboutin, Hermès, Alexander McQueen, Zegna, Carolina Herrera) as well as Ralph Lauren—which counts as practically mundane among the fancier shops—and the ubiquitous Starbucks. It vies with Kansas City's Country Club Plaza for the title of First Shopping Center. As in Los Angeles, valet parkers will take your car for you if you wish and then return it to you. Having a service industry devoted to parking also allows ladies of a certain class and age to leave their cars at the front door of a restaurant and swan in on their high heels to their table. Shopping and dining merge with performance art.

Highland Park Village is a shopping center. People come, they park, they walk around, they shop and eat, and then they go home. We have now moved—as have all large American cities governed by the automobile—beyond that. We now have enclosed malls. These make perfect sense here, in part because of the weather. Who wants to walk outside in summer? Early morning mall walking, well before stores open, is a well-established custom here. Farther from the city, the Galleria, built at the intersection of two major freeways and anchored by large hotels, constitutes a self-enclosed world: multiplex movie theater, ice-skating rink, restaurants, and shops. When it opened in 1982, I wandered into the Dallas branch of San Francisco's Gump's one August morning, dressed in Dallas's summer uniform of shorts and T-shirt (always a mistake in a land where entering movie theaters, not to mention supermarkets, requires layers of clothing). A soignée woman who would have felt at home on the Rue St.-Honoré greeted me and my partner in a resonant, plummy contralto voice: "Welcome, gentlemen, to the Crystal Room at Gump's."

Here is God's plenty. For anyone who thinks of shopping as a significant and pleasurable activity—I am not one, but I have many friends who find this a nice way to pass their time—Dallas will vie with Paris and Los Angeles. I think back to my first visit to the Uffizi Gallery in Florence thirty years ago. Leaving the museum behind two American college girls, I overheard one turn to the other and say, "Oh my God, if the museums here are this good, can you imagine what the shopping is going to be like?"

She was right, of course. Where there is wealth, there is also culture, however one wishes to define it. The Medici understood the irresistible, powerful combination of will, taste, money, and patronage. What happened in Renaissance Florence set the pattern for Gilded Age Manhattan and then, a century later, for Texas. If Henry James and Edith Wharton had lived into the late twentieth century, they would have found the plate tectonics of Texas society not unlike those of their New York and Newport. "Old money" here means fifty years; "new money" means yesterday.

This is still, in endearingly curious ways, a small town in which everyone knows everyone else. Intimacies work on smaller and larger scales. Some years ago, entertaining a visiting job candidate at a local French restaurant, I noticed a quartet of diners moving across the room toward my table. They stopped to greet me, and I made the necessary introductions: "Let me present Irina Dumitrescu, who is visiting from New Haven. This is Mr. and Mrs. Denker, and Mr. and Mrs. Perot." The Yale graduate student was first incredulous, then impressed. "You know Ross Perot?" she asked. She accepted our job offer.

Gossip columnists revel in the misbehavior of the nouveaux riches. Everyone in the last century knew that H. L. Hunt had several families. Everyone today can watch the antics of Mark Cuban on television. Murders among the social set get the full attention of the local press. Even more modest peccadilloes, like the plastic surgery and purported womanizing of Jerry Jones, the owner of the Dallas Cowboys, who could give Silvio Berlusconi a run for his money, or shoplifting by a Dallas socialite, warrant page 1 coverage.

A local observer once said that all it takes to break into Dallas society is a tuxedo and ten thousand dollars. That was in the 1950s. The cost has risen (add several more zeros to the number), but the principle still obtains. As in Manhattan, charity balls raise not only money but also the social cachet of the benefactors.

In the late 1990s, my aunt and uncle, both professional musicians, visited me when they came to town for a music educators' convention. They had traveled extensively through Europe and Asia, but when I met them for dinner, following their tours of art museums, private collections, and the new concert hall, they gasped, "Now we understand where all the money has gone." What downtrodden Philadelphia, my hometown, on a decline since 1950, had been trying to accomplish for years, Dallas could do virtually overnight. When the real estate magnate Trammell Crow decided in the mid-1990s to build a home for the best of his thousands of pieces of Asian art, he simply called his children together and told them he was planning to spend a couple million dollars of their inheritance to establish the Trammell and Margaret Crow Collection of Asian Art, situated between the Morton H. Meyerson Symphony Center (for the construction of which Ross Perot gave ten million dollars on the stipulation that it be named for the president of his company) and the Dallas Museum of Art. It is a little jewel box of wonders located between two giants.

Later, Raymond Nasher, a transplanted Bostonian who married a Dallas girl, wondered what to do with the important collection of modern sculpture he and his late wife had amassed over forty years. Courted by museums here and abroad, he finally did the right thing and gave his collection to the city where he had made his fortune in real estate. He commissioned a masterpiece from Renzo Piano. Who paid for it? He did, of course. So did the Perot family, when they donated the new downtown Perot Museum of Nature and Science. If you want something done right, do it yourself. The entrepreneurial spirit, when combined with a sense of noblesse oblige, has a lot to recommend it. Among other things, you can circumvent nasty red tape.

It has taken Dallas a while to realize that the arts are good for business, as well as vice versa. The story goes that a former mayor, himself a wealthy man, when asked to support the fledgling Dallas Civic Opera in the late 1950s (Maria Callas appeared in its first production, at the height of her career and notoriety), said, "I'll pay anything to support the opera as long as I don't have to go to it." Many men of means say the same to their wives about society balls: they'll pay double *not* to go to the party but stay home instead. Few eastern or old-world bigwigs have the confidence or naïveté to make their prejudices known with such unabashed exuberance. The Dallas Symphony, well into its second century, has had almost as many lives as a cat, if not the phoenix. Now safely housed, since 1989, in a hall acclaimed for its acoustics and design, it is unlikely to go away again, although it suffers from many of the problems—occasional deficits, graying audiences, unimaginative programming, half-empty houses—common to most American orchestras, many of which are in far worse shape.

The visual arts have had their share of controversy as well as success. In the 1950s, right-wingers attacked Picasso as a Communist sympathizer when the art museum mounted an exhibition. In the 1970s, a Henry Moore sculpture in front of a new city hall designed by I. M. Pei drew abusive criticism. (But so did a work by Richard Serra in lower Manhattan.) Art can be bought and sold. It therefore does well under capitalism. Living with beautiful things, as Mary McCarthy once observed, may not necessarily increase one's ethical, moral, or political sympathies, but it does keep the economy moving and gives badges of honor to the people with sufficient income to buy, or even commission, works of art.

All of this hardly means that an American aesthetic has traditionally fared well here, aside from the ubiquitous delight in cowboy art, from the most sophisticated Remingtons and Russells in Fort Worth's Amon Carter Museum as well as private local collections to garden-variety bulls, broncos, and mustangs that dot the landscape. Until recently, private collectors have gone in for French impressionism and eighteenth-century English painting, and they have done their houses in ancien régime or British manorial style. American furniture has done less well. When I bought my prairie-style house in the 1970s, an architect friend from California told me to find pieces by the Stickleys or Greene & Greene, of whom I had never heard. I began looking. In Dallas, mission furniture was not on the radar screen; it had long since been shipped away as being of little value or interest. Pretty soon, celebrity collectors like Calvin Klein and Barbra Streisand put American arts and crafts furniture back on the map and out of the reach of ordinary buyers.

The recent series of excellent public buildings in Dallas (city hall, concert hall, museums) has been matched by a small number of forward-looking residential ones. The few ultramodern or aesthetically daring houses stand out in a landscape of predictable choices. Perhaps it is like this everywhere. Architecturally, the Dallas bourgeoisie has always played it safe, first with mansard roofs (one tale has it that a roof was put on upside down in the 1950s and no one noticed) on pseudo-French chalets, more recently with Georgian piles, bedecked with out-of-scale Palladian ornaments and unnecessary decorative shutters. Spanish colonial has made a comeback during the past decade. The McMansions stand cheek by jowl on small plots in the highly desirable part of town called Highland Park, a self-enclosed suburb like Brookline within Boston or Beverly Hills in Los Angeles, around which the city has grown. The "homes" (real estate agents never call a house a "house"; even apartments are marketed as "apartment homes") must be both spanking new and stylistically conventional. Any house with a library, a real room with built-in shelves for books, is not a new

house. Game rooms, media rooms, rooms with pool tables, are easier to find.

One set of friends moved to Dallas from Paris in 2008 to take
up work as art historians. Somehow they would have to accommodate the collections from their *hôtel particulier* on the Boulevard St.-
Germain. For them, this was no problem. They took themselves to
the local IKEA and got ready-made shelving. Their French relatives,
coming to visit at Christmas, were naturally impressed by the new
house, by the backyard pool, and especially by the size, elegance,
and number of the bathrooms. It was, I suppose, ever thus: every
culture craves and envies what another culture has. Some of my
college friends who had moved to Dallas from Massachusetts at the
same time I did were escorted around by a local real estate agent
who, when they told her they would prefer an older house with
some charm or character, replied bemusedly, "Oh, you mean you
want a used home?" They supposed they did.

The recent mania—"Georgian on My Mind"?—infects more
than residential real estate. In the same upscale neighborhood of
Highland Park, my university, founded in 1911, has developed a
campus that took its original design and shape from Thomas Jefferson's for the University of Virginia. The perfect, modest rotunda
in Charlottesville, harking back to the Pantheon in Rome, is an
exquisite building bounded at right angles by small arcaded dormitories extending along the length of a green. In Texas, bigger is
usually thought better. The optimistic, confident founders of SMU
not only imitated the Jefferson rotunda but also enlarged it: the
university's first building sits at the top of a small incline and commands a campus filled with Georgian buildings, some of which are
enormous, others more modest in scale. These include everything:
parking garages, gymnasium, football stadium, dormitories, and
classrooms, all constructed of red brick unrelieved by ivy or orna-
ment other than the entirely unnecessary columns and pilasters that
announce to passersby, "We are an institution of higher learning."

Like all university architectural idioms—the faux Gothic of Princeton and Duke, the faux Georgian of Harvard's 1930s residential houses, the mishmash of Yale—SMU's Herculean-Georgian takes a symbolic stand with its chosen architectural leitmotif, in this case a deeply conservative one.

When the university recently built a new museum for its small, excellent collection of Spanish art donated by the late oilman Algur Meadows, it might have commissioned something extraordinary or at least unusual. Many forward-looking locals hoped that the university would extend an invitation to Santiago Calatrava, to whom it had just given an arts award. Instead, Calatrava contributed only a single work, a sculpture-fountain whose rising and falling metal beams hypnotically mimic the movement of a wave. This piece stands in front of the aggressively Georgian museum that looks like a mausoleum perched atop a parking garage. The shiny, steely, modern fountain in fact seems out of place. My university's trustees, many of them Dallas burghers, will take risks in business but seldom in artistic matters. All universities now commit themselves to the idea of diversity in education. We want diverse student populations and more varied curricula. But my school also insists on keeping up an architectural homogeneity. A manicured, uniform campus—however beautiful—has meaning, intended or not.

The university trustees and supporters like to use the label "traditional," instead of "conservative" or "conventional," to describe their aesthetic preferences. These preferences reflect the prevailing political views of the city fathers, the ruling class. Although Texas has always had a strong populist tradition—kept alive by *The Texas Observer* and, until her death, the journalist Molly Ivins—Dallas has been fairly immune to it. The city of Dallas, with its increasing Hispanic population, votes Democratic, as does Houston, but Texas suburbs and gerrymandered districting keep Republican politicians in office. Although the city has successfully moved beyond its post-1963 shame, older citizens can still remember with embarrassment that this is where Adlai Stevenson was spat upon and where the John Birch Society had strong local support. Racial conflicts that sometimes literally burned through other American cities in the 1960s merely simmered here; to its credit, Dallas ended de jure if not de facto segregation quietly. It was better for business as well as the city's reputation. Enlightened leaders like the late mayor Erik Jonsson and the late merchant prince Stanley Marcus helped the city recover from its status as international pariah. In 2013, marking the fiftieth anniversary of the Kennedy assassination, some Dallasites still felt a need to make amends. Others pointed out that where Buffalo and Washington, D.C., are never held responsible for the deaths of Presidents McKinley, Lincoln, and Garfield, the city of Dallas, not Lee Harvey Oswald alone, shares the blame for what happened here. Larry McMurtry, the unofficial literary spokesman for contemporary as well as mythic Texas, has had a longtime aversion to Dallas, which he has labeled "a city run by and for bankers. This is good if you are a banker. If not, not."

Dallas is, in ways that New York is not, America itself. Dallas—how many new American cities are different?—can now be defined by its commitment to big-time sports and big-time religion. To say that sport is religion is no understatement. Whenever an academic like me tries to persuade university administrators that spending more money on pseudo-professional teams (read: football) is like pouring money down a drain, or observes that every defense for Division I athletics (they raise money; they draw attention to the school; they promote school spirit) has been proved categorically untrue, eventually someone will play the trump card: "But this is Texas, and this is football." End of discussion. Whenever the Dallas Cowboys play in the Super Bowl—not that they have done so in years—the city's water pressure plummets during television commercials, because everyone goes to the bathroom and flushes the toilet at the same time.

Some years ago, I used to frequent a barbershop, not a posh

unisex salon, but an old-fashioned place with fluorescent lights; high, plumped revolving leather chairs; manicurists who called everyone "Hon"; and paunchy, affable heterosexual good-ole-boy barbers who wore jeans and cowboy belt buckles and who did not take long to give a haircut. One Tuesday, my barber asked me whether I'd seen Troy Aikman's winning touchdown pass in the Monday night Cowboys game. I confessed that I hadn't. Obviously sensing that I was not keeping up my end of the conversation, my barber, Dwayne, said, "Oh, I guess you're not a football fan."

"No," I replied, "not really."

"You watch baseball, then?"

"No, I'm sorry, I don't follow baseball, either."

"Wait, son, if you don't like football and you don't like baseball, what do you like?"

I hesitated, not really thinking, and blurted out naively, "Opera." Only the sound of a pair of scissors hitting the floor broke the silence.

Even a non-observing, non-believing person cannot avoid noticing the pervasiveness of religion throughout the region. Although the entire Bible Belt has expanded, encircling the girth of much of the country, Dallas may be the buckle of the belt. Roadside churches, billboards, advertisements, meet the eye everywhere. For more than a month around Easter, sometimes even longer, ritzy Highland Park lawns sport tasteful little crosses planted in the front yards proclaiming, "He Is Risen!" It's enough to make a secular person cringe. When I was growing up, religion was a private affair. Now it is unashamedly and evangelically public, touting not only a message but also an affirmation of the good faith of the believers, who are patting themselves on the back.

Like our southern presidents "Jimmy" Carter and "Bill" Clinton, preachers usually dispense with all formality now. America has abandoned or at least suspended last names. The South has led the way. There's Dr. Jim, Reverend Don, Father Steve, Pastor

Wally, not to mention Jerry Falwell and Jimmy Swaggart. Large posters with pictures of these smiling men of God with their pressed hair dot the local freeways.

The United States now prides itself on being a land more than friendly to religion, especially friendly religion. Southern hospitality has become the national religious custom: "Y'all come back, y'hear?" "Y'all don't make strangers of yourselves." Religion, all-inclusive, nonthreatening, welcomes and draws us in, like big potluck picnics. On the side of the laity, "Sunday best" now means ironed jeans and starched shirts for tieless men, although their womenfolk hew—at church as in the workplace—to a less relaxed standard. As Americans have come to profess their faiths more openly, they have become more casual in their rituals. Fear and Trembling have made way for Hugs and High Fives. Religion Lite has become the equivalent of low-cal, low-carb diets, especially in the happy planting of spirituality in the suburbs. What would Jesus do? In Dallas, he would probably live in a new house, drive an SUV, coach his kids' soccer team, and greet people at Sunday services by stretching out his mighty hand and asking, "Hi! How y'all doin'?" Pope Francis must have been paying attention, when making his cold calls, to his Protestant brethren.

Let me be fair: It's not just the mainstream Christians who have felt the pull of convenience and ease. Some years ago, a local couple, the age of my parents, invited me to join them for Kol Nidre services at the most prominent reform synagogue in Dallas, the largest Jewish congregation in the South. Because on the holiest night of the religious calendar the congregation overflows the sanctuary's seating capacity, Temple Emanu-El has two services. My hosts suggested we make our appearance at the earlier one, after which we would go out for an elegant Italian dinner (rather than the traditional at-home Jewish meal of roast chicken or pot roast). "Thank you so much," I said, "but even I know that you're supposed to eat before sundown and then go to shul and fast for twenty-four hours."

"Oh, yes," they smilingly allowed, "but this will be much more fun." Who was I to complain? When in Dallas . . .

And when in Dallas, one eats Dallas foods as well as eating on a Dallas schedule. We now have our share of artisanal cheeses, micro-breweries, expensive chewy bread, gleaming organic produce, and international specialties. Whole Foods got its start in Austin; Dallas was one of its first venues outside the Hill Country. South American, Indian, Vietnamese, Middle Eastern, and African markets exist in neighborhood pockets. Forty-five years ago, all store-bought bread was of the Wonder sort, soft and tasteless, and lettuce meant iceberg. Liquor by the glass was not available in restaurants; you had to become a member for a nominal fee. Not any longer. We have become international, and "ethnic" means more than Tex-Mex. Where once we had only the mystique of Coors beer—made from the purest water in the Rocky Mountains and never sold east of the Mississippi—we now have home brew that actually tastes like something.

Modifications, especially in pronunciation, have been made. The universal flaky French breakfast pastry is referred to as a "crah-sant" (as it is almost everywhere). No amount of correction will succeed in getting a Dallasite's mouth around the actual word. I have also given up my efforts to get the staff at delicatessens to change the signs reading "proscuitto" to "prosciutto." Or to remind the uninterested, unaware cafeteria and coffeehouse student personnel that an Italian sandwich is called a "panino," not a "panini," as they say here and—well—virtually everywhere in America. And, likewise, that a single cookie is not a "biscotti," or two of them "biscottis." Linguists can explain these changes as the natural Americanization of a Romance language. I still don't like them. Call me a dinosaur.

Linguistic purists will wince, but I have softened in my disapproval even as the words and sounds still strike me as tinny. A biscotto by any other name will taste as sweet anywhere you eat it. Still, the availability of asparagus out of season, and of international foods everywhere, and the post–Alice Waters sophistication of the American palate have had, as a downside, the effect of making a middle-aged person or a senior citizen as nostalgic for the comfort foods and watering holes of yore as he is for the old accents that have been absorbed by the blandness of standard American. In Dallas, culinary nostalgia means a yearning for sweets and fats, the favored food groups, and cafeterias, the preferred locale of all social strata, especially after church on Sunday or on cook's night out during the week. (Some people still have cooks.) When the Zodiac Room at Neiman Marcus reached its zenith as the ne plus ultra of culinary art in the mid-1950s, a glutinously sweet poppy seed dressing was the covering of choice for both green and fruit salads. Even today, in our more refined condition, the bottomless glass of iced tea goes with everything, all the time. Tea in a pot must be ordered as "hot tea"; "tea," *tout simple*, means the ubiquitous Drink of the South, available in varying degrees of sweetness.

To someone like me, who grew up with and in the East Coast's Horn and Hardarts—both the Automat and the cafeteria—the grandeur of Texas cafeterias was awe-inspiring. The old drill was standard. The line began with "congeals," an all-purpose label embracing wedges of iceberg lettuce, deviled eggs, Waldorf salads, ambrosia, aspics, and Jell-O molds of extraordinary complexity and variety. It progressed through main dishes that included southern hash, a succulent mixture of brisket and onions, and proceeded to bitter greens (collard, mustard), four kinds of cooked okra, yellow squash casserole topped with cornflakes, and overcooked green beans that you had to avoid at all costs. Then you came to the section for breads, including yeasty white rolls that emitted a puff of steam when you opened them and corn bread that remained moist and did not crumble. The line ended with desserts that would have inspired Wayne Thiebaud paintings: the pies—cherry, coconut, banana cream, other fruits in season—plain yellow cake, multi-layered German chocolate cake, and some puddings. A high-class place used whipped cream; a less attentive one, some chemical imitation. And iced tea accompanied everything.

Local food, *la cocina tejana*, has at least one pinnacle, which many scorn but which I adore: chicken-fried steak. The best version used to be served at a now defunct lunchtime-only cafeteria near downtown. The restaurant's motto: "We Cook for Texans, Not Frenchmen." After thirty-five years of waking up at four in the morning, shopping at the farmers' market, opening the doors, doing the cooking, cleaning up, and getting home at four in the after-noon, the tired owners announced they were closing their shop. Their announcement initiated a month of local mourning. During the final week, the lines snaked around the block; people like me took pictures of our last meal. Tears were shed. Jane and Michael Stern, tireless aficionados of American diner food, touted the place in *Roadfood and Goodfood*, and no one ever ate more chicken-fried steak than these two well-traveled, well-fed Yankees.

The concept is simple, but the proper execution can be tricky: you bang to death a thin piece of meat of not very high quality, you batter it with what you normally use for fried chicken, you fry it quickly to sear in the steak's juices, and you serve it with a rich, creamy, peppery gravy, accompanied with homemade mashed po-tatoes and greens with a strong iron taste. In bad places, the gravy looks and tastes like wallpaper glue. For dessert? *La pièce de résis-tance*: peanut butter pie, silky, lacy, in a crust made with lard and covered with whipped cream. And one never expected to go back to the office for a full afternoon of hard labor: a two-hour siesta was called for, plus an additional dose of Lipitor and/or an arterial vacuuming. Texas food will not qualify as part of anyone's low-fat, low-sodium, or low-carb regimen. As in other areas of local culture, nothing succeeds like excess.

I am no expert, but I must offer a modest word regarding the two most popular local cuisines, Tex-Mex and barbecue, subjects about which people have said a great deal, spilled much ink, and raised many hackles. The first is a hybrid affair that deserves more respect in an age of hyphenated diversities. We distinguish it from California-Mex, which uses more avocados and pretends to be lighter and healthier; from New Mexico–Mex, which substitutes green chilies for our red ones; and from authentic, multifaceted Mexican cuisine, in which the black bean, rather than the brown *pinto frijole*, predominates. Redoubtable Tex-Mex has promoted a cuisine of poverty to respectability. Beans, chilies, and onions lend a Texas accent to brisket, rather than pork or other cuts of beef. When I moved to Texas from Boston, where brisket was available mostly in Jewish neighborhoods, I took heart when I learned that it was a staple throughout gentile Dallas. More recently, Dallas can lay claim to having invented fajitas, not an authentic Mexican dish at all, and the frozen margarita, a distinctly *yanqui* concoction. (On another front, in 1951 a local secretary invented Liquid Paper in her garage to help her undo her too frequent typing mistakes. Texas ingenuity knows no bounds.)

A related north-of-the-Rio-Grande-food cuisine, barbecue has inspired partisans and combatants throughout the South. Experts call it vitamin Q. People take sides. This is serious business, or "bidnis" as they say down here. Do you use pork or brisket? In Texas, only brisket. Pulled, shredded, sliced, chopped? What kind of wood for the smoking? At what temperature and for how long? What, if any, kind of sauce? A dry marinade or a wet one? A small west Texas ghost town, Terlingua, hosts an annual chili cook-off. Football is not the only thing to produce intense competitive rivalry.

Barbecue has made forays into the hipper precincts of Brooklyn and elsewhere throughout the States. Regardless of how you like it, the point of barbecue is that it is messy. The worldliest, most sophisticated hosts know to take out-of-town, especially international, guests to the little roadside shacks that have the best stuff. Or even to serve it at home on fine china. Just as Franklin and Eleanor Roosevelt gave hot dogs to King George and Queen Elizabeth when the royals visited Hyde Park, so our local gentry, taking their cue from the late Stanley Marcus, always do the Texas thing for our visitors. Several years ago, I had to entertain a prominent New York writer coming to give a reading. I asked whether she would prefer an elegant continental meal or down and dirty barbecue. "How could you even ask that question, Willard?" she replied. Stanley Marcus was an arbiter of fashion in more than couture. Why, after all, give your guests *quenelles de brochet sauce Nantua*, *coulibiac de saumon*, or *veau Prince Orloff*, those tired old-world masterpieces?

At the 1989 opening of the Meyerson Symphony Center, a glamorous local philanthropist threw a meal for visiting music and architecture critics at her pink mansion. It was late August, not Dallas's most promising or hospitable season. The temperature as well as the humidity hovered in the mid-nineties, but we ate buffet-style, al fresco, under the fragrant magnolias. The spread: barbecue, pinto beans, three types of coleslaw, corn bread, fried okra, and pecan pie, all washed down with bottles of Lone Star beer and pitchers of iced tea. The press could not get enough of it. Journalists are not known for delicacy or fastidiousness to start with, but I knew that our hostess had made the right choice when I saw celebrated British and German music critics jostling and pushing one another to get back in line for seconds and thirds. Barbecue sauce covered shirts and ties, jackets having long since been removed. "I learned this from Stanley," the hostess said to me. The Old World reveled in its collision or collaboration with the Wild West. We were locavores before the word had gained its current cachet.

Thinking about a place inevitably means thinking of *any* place, of the idea of place itself and its relationship to human identity. Some people feel at home everywhere, some people nowhere. Most of us have greater attachments to some places than to others, for reasons ranging from habit to aesthetic preferences. My thoughts, above, about Dallas began with bodily things—details of temperature and humidity—and ended with food. Eating is also of the body. Wallace Stevens wrote, "Beauty is momentary in the mind . . . / But in the flesh it is immortal." He is suggesting the difficulty of registering, on the pulses of memory, a memory of and from the senses. The body constantly receives messages, but the mind, that poor sieve, retains only a faint recollection of the shape of an experience. Amy Clampitt once remarked that only a person who knew what it was like, deep in her bones, to be cold could fully appreciate Keats's "Eve of St. Agnes" and its opening in the bitter chill of a January night. But once winter has passed, did Clampitt, or Keats, or any "Snow Man" really recall that chill? Does the body have a mind of its own? Thinking back to an experience, can I say, "*This* is what happened"? I know, in my mind, that I have felt Dallas heat and its effects on body and spirit, the ways it debilitates, irritates, and fatigues me as cold never can. The recalled pleasures of certain foods stick with me after their tastes have vanished. Wordsworth makes an odd, provocative distinction in *The Prelude*: "the soul, / Remembering *how* she felt, but *what* she felt / Remembering not" (italics mine). It is as though this great poet of childhood were saying something like "I knew that I was happy but I cannot remember what happiness was, or even what it was like." The process of remembering takes precedence over nameable feelings.

Whenever I leave Dallas—during summers, on sabbaticals, or even for shorter periods—I do not see it in color, only in black and white or sepia, in my mind's eye; in spite of glaring sun and primary colors, it never comes clear within my imaginative faculties the way that Venice, Paris, London, New York, Boston, and Philadelphia do. It has been reduced, minimized. Perhaps, incredulous, I have not really accepted the fact that Dallas has been my home for most of my life. Why do those cities I have visited on vacation, or inhabited in the ever-receding past, loom larger in my dreams? How can this be? Is it the result of weather, architecture, topography, distance from family and other loved ones, of a preference for gray New England chill or the Old World of stone, great-rooted blossoming chestnut trees, and urban squares with children playing near fountains? A deep fondness for a land with four distinct seasons or—in New England at least—five of them, with "mud season" sandwiched between winter and spring? The absence of pedestrian life in Dallas, the omnipresence of the automobile and of what Robert Lowell called the "savage servility [that] slides by on grease"? Some strong sympathy with the poet Frank O'Hara, who claimed that he was always made a little nervous when he could not have a subway sign clearly in view? The inevitable recurrence to scenes of childhood, to native soil that holds anyone's roots?

All of the above?

For all the clichés about southern friendliness and New York brusqueness or Bostonian chill, it seems to me that any city in which people bump up against one another on the streets is ipso facto more humane than one in which they merely see one another waiting in air-conditioned cars at stoplights.

In the nineteenth century, during the late high-water years of the British Empire, soldiers, clergymen, administrators, doctors, scientists, businessmen, and other adventurers, some with families, went to India to serve the Raj. If they did not die there, go native, or otherwise take leave of their senses, they often returned to England, to live out the remainder of their days obscurely in quiet seaside towns, the kind you read about in Trollope novels, retired from the distant place that was, in most cases, the strangest and most memorable they had ever seen. Often they felt entirely out of place when they came back to their nominal home. Their destination did not match their point of origin, even though it was technically the same. Or perhaps they were not the same people they had been when they had embarked years before.

It took at least three decades for me to learn how to answer the question "Where are you from?"

"I'm from Philadelphia," I now say, "but I live in Dallas." Later, I awoke one morning with the right metaphor for my life: I am stationed here. A person who is stationed somewhere really belongs nowhere. Or perhaps he belongs everywhere. A mild sense of alienation hardly distinguishes my case from that of countless contemporaries. Intellectuals, artists, and academics probably belong nowhere to begin with. We are quasi- if not genuine expatriates, with a tendency to look inward to the worlds of literature and thought. Universities, wherever they are, are all self-contained microcosms that resemble one another more than any other kind of community. My academic department houses many New Yorkers and other northeasterners, but only one native Texan. We came to Dallas from somewhere else.

My academic tour of duty will end soon. I shall probably return to my equivalent of the Englishman's seaside retirement home, cohabiting with my partner of four decades, from whom I have been separated for reasons of employment for much of the time. Perhaps we'll marry. We don't want to rush into anything.

Will I return "home"? What does this mean? Elizabeth Bishop makes an existential point at the end of the title poem of her 1965 volume, *Questions of Travel*. Her traveler—herself, really—jots down three, far from rhetorical, questions in a notebook:

> *"Is it lack of imagination that makes us come*
> *to imagined places, not just stay at home?*

Or could Pascal have been not entirely right
about just sitting quietly in one's room?

Continent, city, country, society:
the choice is never wide and never free.
And here, or there . . . No. Should we have stayed at home,
wherever that may be?"

Blaise Pascal felt dread at what he called the eternal silence of infinite spaces, a dread that Robert Frost calls up in his grimly chatty poem "Desert Places." The French philosopher also implied that most people have a fear of sitting quietly in a room. The American poet remarks that he has it in himself "so much nearer home / To scare myself with my own desert places." Between cosmic traumas and domestic itchiness hovers the urge to travel, to see the world, to move away, to get out of oneself. Peace abides, with contentment, always out of sight, elsewhere, not here. Bishop, who experienced domestic pleasures in direct proportion to deeper anxieties, understood that neither home nor abroad, neither the life upon native terrain nor that in "imagined" or actual foreign places, can exist without a doubled sense of life's transience and of intense, specifically local charms. Wherever one finds oneself, one is always at sea, because something seems missing. We belong nowhere, and therefore everywhere. Horace's "coelum non animum mutant qui trans mare currunt" (those who race across the ocean are changing their skies, not their souls) means, as does Bishop's final question above, that "here" and "there" are equally real and equally fictive ideas.

Life, wherever and however we may lead it, is a pilgrimage lived in the present. When the literary scholar Hugh Kenner left a teaching post at the University of California in Santa Barbara, having worked there for two decades, he decamped for another position, on the East Coast. A solicitous friend asked him, "How does it feel leaving Santa Barbara?" To which the eminent man quickly replied, "Like checking out of a motel." He had not felt at home. Perhaps he never felt at home anywhere. Home, "wherever that may be," as Bishop sums it up, is neither where we came from nor where we are going but an image we carry with us. Always, we remain unmoored.

I have never felt so unmoored, unconnected yet exhilarated, and so fully myself, as when I went to Japan.

JAPAN 🍃

When I went to Japan, my biggest worry was neither jet lag nor culture shock, not food poisoning, not the fear of getting lost. After all, at a certain age one doesn't sleep well to begin with, so a twelve-hour flight will wreak little somatic havoc. Unlike China and India, Japan is modern, compact, and civilized, regimented and industrialized in a way that makes it seem the most American of Asian cultures. All appliances work there. Most of ours have been made there. Sushi and tempura, not to mention green teas, tofu, soba, and udon, have become staples of our Western diet, so I knew that nothing terrible, or even surprising, was going to slide down my throat. It's a small country, and I was going to be in only two cities. I knew that I wasn't going to be stranded.

It was the language that kept me up at night.

I have always been a proud polyglot. Perfectly useless Latin and Greek, schoolboy German, opera-and-menu-and-Dante-inflected Italian, and more than passable French have seen me through.

Spanish, the language that would be most practical—both at home and internationally—somehow passed me by. (In junior high school when we started signing up for language study, the unwritten rule was that the best students learned Latin, the least talented Spanish. I was a snob.) Still, with a kind of Romance Esperanto at my disposal, and with a combination of facility, enthusiasm, and the unself-conscious ability to blurt things out without thinking about correctness, I have stumbled through Spain and Portugal, as well as Germany, France, and Italy, managing jokes in languages I knew poorly, like the one about W. C. Fields and his reason for not drinking water.

And in Bayreuth one October afternoon, an hour after arriving, and following a grueling transatlantic flight followed by a long train ride, I walked around the small town and, when approached by two middle-aged German women asking for directions to the Old Castle, answered correctly in their native tongue. I had just looked at the map to gain my bearings, and some vestigial words from German 101 miraculously came out of my mouth. Delighted and self-congratulating, I then took myself out for a beer.

But I had never gone to a country where I would be unable to speak, read, or understand a single word. In a literary academic like me, this prospect instilled both fear and a sense of challenge. My idea of adventure has never included trekking through the Sahara, scaling high mountains, freezing in the Arctic, or shooting into outer space. My body takes care of itself in temperate climes well enough, and I can take my exercise in modest, unthreatening ways. Excitement has always meant getting along in a different culture with enough language for everyday transactions.

Learning Japanese was something for which I was entirely unprepared. Now I understand why we call such things foreign languages. I looked at phrase books. Not a cognate to be found anywhere; nothing mnemonic to lead me through the meanings of the words. No clue as to which part of a sentence was the verb and which the subject. I have—or rather had, age having begun to take its inevitable mental as well as physical toll—a gift for languages. I used to be able to review irregular verbs—moods, tenses, and all—on a long plane ride from one side of the pond to the other.

Not this time. I have always shuddered when hearing my countrymen abroad begin, without an "excuse me" or a "by your leave," to speak English to everyone, on the presumption that they will be understood. (That presumption is of course often accurate.) I always tell my students that wherever they travel, they should learn to say "Good morning," "Good evening," "I do not speak [here fill in the relevant language]," "Do you speak English?" and "Where is the bathroom?" These five will get you through almost any situation, and the last one I have always found particularly useful. "Please," "Thank you," and "Excuse me" add the necessary note of deferential politesse.

With the help of Japanese-speaking American friends and a phrase book, I finally mastered them all. "Sumimasen, nihongo dekimasen; eigo ga hanasemasu ka?" became my password, my talisman, my open sesame every step of the way. "Excuse me, I do not speak Japanese; do you speak English?" I felt simultaneously humbled and inspired. On the one hand, most of the people I encountered were academics or worked in the service industry, in hotels, restaurants, shops, museums, and shrines. They either had some English or could direct me to a nearby colleague or coworker who did. On the other, and more important, hand, the very fact of making oneself helpless, childlike, and passive, and having to depend on the assistance of others, meant that I became, even more than in a "foreign" country like England where the bond of a common language eases cultural exchanges, entirely on the qui vive, alert to everything and everyone in the surround.

My linguistic deficiencies in Japanese came with attendant disappointments as well as pleasing surprises. My primary, or at least nominal, reason for going to Japan in the first place was to deliver academic lectures, before three university audiences, on the subject of American poetry. Two of these were in the form of seminars for graduate students. Once I surveyed the scene and realized that their comprehension was not quite total, I simply slowed the pace, improvised, gesticulated, and tried to amuse them. But because the Japanese seem to equate professionalism with tedium and expect their teachers to maintain a pomposity appropriate to their venerability, I am not sure how far I got with light, bright Anglo-American sparkle.

For my final engagement, at Tokyo Women's University, which thinks of itself as the Wellesley of Japan, my host had asked me to talk about the origins of modern American poetry in Dickinson, Poe, and Whitman before an audience of 140 third-year female English students. This would not be a problem, I assured her. But it became clear after two minutes that the majority of the audience probably understood little of what I was saying. Readjusting quickly, I decided upon a slower pace. I eliminated all of my prepared remarks. Many of the young women had turned on their recording devices. By the end, many were busy on their cell phones, either taking notes or, more likely, texting their girlfriends. Some were dozing, others chatting. I later asked another professor what the point of my exercise had been. She replied, helpfully, "It's always important for the students to hear English, especially poetry, read clearly and beautifully." An American reading out loud: that was my role. A recording would have served as well, but I managed to get through my allotted time with minimal embarrassment.

"Wait," I asked myself, "how different are these kids from American students who really do understand their native language but who often are not giving full notice to what their professor is saying?" "Plus ça change," in other words, or "mutatis mutandis," or whatever one might say in Japanese, students are pretty much the same the world over. Such was my thought not so much at the time as afterward.

The most compelling revelations always come to travelers in the most ordinary situations. Every transaction in a foreign country becomes an adventure: "Oh, this is how to buy a train ticket." "Now I can make a phone call." "They drive on the left? Who knew?" Elizabeth Bishop put it well in a charming poem, "Arrival at Santos," about a visit to Brazil that led her into a period of expatriation she had never anticipated. (An allergic reaction forced her into a hospital. She met a woman who became her lover, and stayed for almost two decades.) Everything seems unexpected and mundane simultaneously:

> So that's the flag. I never saw it before.
> I somehow never thought of there *being* a flag,
>
> but of course there was, all along. And coins, I presume,
> and paper money; they remain to be seen.

One's eyes are open in ways they seldom are at home.

Years ago, with a colleague from my university's art history department, I led a score of well-heeled, worldly, sophisticated middle-aged travelers on what we billed as an art-and-culture week in London. Midwinter meant a slow, post–New Year's tourist season, easy-to-get tickets for operas, concerts, and plays, and reasonable rates at the Russell, a faded dowager of a Bloomsbury hotel from the Edwardian era. What many of our adult campers most remembered about their trip upon their return Stateside was that—regardless of how many times they had been to Britain previously—this was the first time that they had actually ridden the Tube. Previously pampered by drivers and tour guides, or too timid to take the subway on their own, these Texans happily became, if only for a holiday, ordinary people. And ordinariness is what we experience when we travel.

Japan opened my ears, eyes, and mind in more dramatic but also more subtle ways. Banality has a lot to recommend it. As in all

travel, everything boils down to sameness and difference: the recognition that *they* and their world resemble us and ours, and also do
not. Because language comes at us through both eye and ear, through
what we see and what we hear, linguistic retrieval and experience
become more allied with general sensuous vigilance abroad than at
home. Everything is to be read. Everything is to be heard. Every
phenomenon, in the country Roland Barthes called an "empire of
signs," demands unpacking.

Not only an empire: an elaborate display, which the attentive,
or even the casual, tourist cannot help thinking is intentional, even
though it may not be. Here come some sumo wrestlers, like so many
French geese or ducks, force-fed so their livers will fatten and stuffed
to the bursting point. The big guys cannot really walk, only waddle
and shuffle through lines of photograph-snapping sidewalk crowds
into the stadium for their brief afternoon matches. What do they
mean? How does one read them? Like everyone else in Tokyo,
they seem to be on parade. And it's not just the wrestlers but also
their diametrical opposites, the geishas, arriving at sunset for their
appointed assignations, modest but at the same time aware that all
eyes are on them. Or the swans of Ginza, gorgeous Japanese Au-
drey Hepburn look-alikes, thin, long-necked, elegant, coiffed, and
pearled, going to work or to shop. And the kids in Takeshita Street,
like punks the world over, sensitive to fashions different from the
ones I know: the popular look when I visited was part goth, part
Barbie doll, part Alice in Wonderland. These stapled and pierced
teenagers seemed to slouch to a different drummer.

In Japan, fashion looks more serious than it does at home, either
because it really is or merely because a tourist watches more carefully things he might ignore on native ground. He knows the signs
better at home and therefore internalizes or forgets them. What we
do not understand, what we cannot read: this is what strikes us
abroad. A kimono, for example: What does it mean in the twenty-

first century? I saw some ladies, all of a certain age, walking down the street in traditional garb. Perhaps they worked in some industry that demanded the costume. Perhaps they were going to a special event. In Kyoto, geishas wear the kimono but expose the rear of their necks, a traditional erotic spot. In my Tokyo hotel, I saw half a dozen weekend wedding celebrations: some of the older women wore kimonos, but the rest, including all of the younger ones, were garbed in high European chic. Every department store was filled with Armani, Burberry, Ralph Lauren, and other Western boutiques. Banana Republic outlets lined the streets. The culture of 1966, when Barthes made his trip, has been almost entirely transformed. We might have been on Madison Avenue, Rue St.-Honoré, or the Via Tornabuoni. Shopping makes the whole world kin.

The culture of food, in the hotels at least, was equally international. On my first morning in Tokyo, I came down to the dining room eager to try the Japanese breakfast specialties, the nori, miso soup, pickled fish, some unknown gelatinous things, plus accompaniments like the *takuan* and *umeboshi* pickles, and the raw eggs beaten and poured over rice to make golden *tamago kake gohan*. When I looked around, I saw that most of the Japanese guests had chowed down on bacon and eggs or cornflakes and fresh fruit.

Even more daunting than food is the problem of trying to figure out where you are and how to go elsewhere. Tokyo is notorious—like Venice—for the absence or the inscrutability of addresses. Numbers do not move consecutively along a street. Streets often lack signage in either English or Japanese; maps are equally unhelpful. Still, things are better marked than they were fifty years ago when Barthes visited and when he discovered that in order to move from one place to another, he often needed an improvised picture—jotted down by a friend on a piece of paper—with buildings and landmarks drawn in. To reach a certain popular restaurant, a Japanese friend of mine had to tell the taxi driver to head to a specific corner ("Go to the Atré Department Store in Shinjuku and then go one block farther"). Even the locals sometimes cannot figure out directions or know how to get from one place to another.

Barthes claimed that everything in Japan is surface, form, or design. There is no Eastern equivalent for what he would call a "transcendental signified"; that is, things have no deeper or greater meanings than themselves. His general point may exaggerate the idea of cultural difference. The idea of "kata," the form of things, plays a big part in Japanese culture: there is always the correct way of doing something, whether slicing fish or arranging flowers, and it takes years of apprenticeship to master the simplest gestures. This reliance on propriety suggests to a Westerner an almost Platonic idea of form as something eternal and immutable. But Barthes, who could understand Japanese language and culture no better than I, failed to account for the fact that correct form itself signifies an eternal verity. Fascinated by packaging and framing—elegant exteriors that might conceal the most trivial of gifts—Barthes also enthusiastically took the haiku as the representative symbol for everything that happens in Japan. A modest poetic genre, haiku neither defines nor describes (these being characteristic functions of Western poetry or of Western philosophy): it simply is. "The West moistens everything with meaning," he famously observed, but in his eagerness to find in Japanese culture an "exemption from meaning," Barthes was clearly just as guilty of what we now might term "essentializing the other" as any other traveler intent upon understanding both difference and resemblance.

Even more than looking at, and trying to understand, the signs of fashion, I found that the actual language provoked my curiosity. The most enticing, because frustrating, part of the written language is its tripartite systems: the kanji, old Chinese ideograms taken over by the Japanese but pronounced differently; and the hiragana and katakana, both phonetically based and used especially for foreign and new words. Not to mention *romaji,* the Western alphabet freely used. I began to feel modestly proud when one of my hosts showed me the kanji figure for "man," which becomes—with the inclusion of a single horizontal stroke—the figure for "big," and then, with the inclusion of yet a second horizontal stroke, the figure for "heaven." I mastered four or five others as well. These would never suffice to move me beyond nursery school.

Considering that Japanese schoolchildren live on a tightly regulated schedule—so many hundred characters per year throughout school—and that basic newspaper literacy requires the knowledge of several thousand characters, I realized that I would never make the grade. The late Donald Richie, an American writer who lived in Tokyo for almost sixty years, dying there in 2013, and who wrote novels, journalism, books about Japanese culture and especially film, told me at dinner that although he was a fluent speaker, he was also an illiterate and needed people to read the newspaper to him every day. Other Americans have had different and more successful experiences in acquiring reading skills.

However lost I felt—being unable to read, speak, or understand the language—I never sank as low as the sad and lonely Bob Harris, Bill Murray's character in the film *Lost in Translation.* He had virtually no interest in anything around him; I was fascinated by everything. Coming abroad, floating unmoored and loosed from daily habit, only reinforced the deeper alienation and inner unrest his character bore with him everywhere. For him and for Charlotte (Scarlett Johansson), it took an experience of the foreign to reveal the pathos of the everyday, the emptiness within themselves. But a good traveler returns exhilarated, restored, and confirmed by the jolt of strangeness. Not "lost in translation," Robert Frost's famous definition of poetry, but having gained something. Everything comes down to sameness and difference, in life as in language and literature. The literary technique that goes by the name of metaphor is a "carrying-across." The Latin equivalent for this Greek term is, wonderfully, "translation." A thing resembles, or is like, another thing only by virtue of the fact that the two are not identical. Sameness and difference: twin sides of one coin. One culture resembles another as one person resembles another, but each has a unique imprint, DNA, or fingerprint. In art, this uniqueness goes by the name of style, the mark of the maker.

When traveling, one tries to read everything and, as I have said, even the banal gets infused with the exotic just by virtue of existing elsewhere or in a different context. Every tourist comes home impressed by Japanese politeness, cleanliness, punctuality, and deference; trains that run on time and are as tidy as drawing rooms; bathrooms in public places so clean that even the fussiest Western lady will not complain. One giggles at the earnest, often comic attempts to introduce Western foods: bagels, sometimes spelled "bagles," are a staple, but I passed on the soy milk and edamame combo, and the green tea and white chocolate one, that I found at Bagels and Bagels in the food exposition of one major department store.

The eyes are always open abroad. So are the ears. Japanese, to someone who doesn't understand it, is just music, meaningless sounds. Sound in Japan is important, among other reasons, for what it is not. It is seldom loud. The uniformed junior high school students whom I saw marching through national shrines in Kyoto were not only more orderly than their American counterparts; they were also quieter. People do not holler. Voices are not raised. You don't hear cell phones, or people speaking on them, on the subway. This would inconvenience other passengers. It is impolite. (On the street, it's another story; the cell phone has become ubiquitous.) As I wandered through the Kyoto shrine called Kinkaku-ji, the Golden Pavilion, one May morning, I was impressed by these kids, who had both the normal hormone-induced high spirits of thirteen-year-olds on holiday and an adult sense of earnestness in their mission. I was approached twice with requests for information and a photo op. (What kind of assignments do the teachers give their students, and why?)

One shy girl stepped forward and read from a prepared script: "Hello, my name is Yoko. I have been asked to take a picture of a foreigner. What is your name? Where are you from?" Answers duly given, request honored. After a solo shot, I suggested one of Yoko and me, along with some of her chums. The girls giggled, surrounded me, made donkey ears with their fingers, and smiled. Ten minutes later, I repeated the experience, this time with a bunch of boys. Same questions, same photographs. One boy asked me how old I was. When I said sixty-four, they gasped, they bowed, they applauded. How wonderful to be respected for one's height (in my case, a mere five feet eight) and one's age. Never has being a gaijin (foreigner) made me feel so dignified rather than, or in addition to, out of place.

Language often makes us lose our balance. It also, more wonderfully, helps us to regain it. What we hear, what we read, what it all means: it's all words. "What are words?" asked Amy Clampitt as she managed to flirt and communicate on her train ride from the South of France into northern Italy. Everyone can do something similar, at least where the language offers cognates. Not everyone knows a sonnet of Petrarch, let alone Sappho's poetry. Watching television in Assisi once at a hotel, I saw First Lady Nancy Reagan come onto the screen. The hotel landlady made a disparaging remark and then apologized to her American guest. I brushed off her remark. "Signora Reagan è una strega," I muttered. My landlady became my new best friend. As with Clampitt, words themselves give way, like leaves, but we manage to catch something and make it stick between us. Everything changes and everything remains the same. The music, rather than the words, unites the communicating and semi-understanding fellow travelers. By "losing track of language," we can become like Clampitt. The poet gains an even greater sense of herself and her relations with other human beings.

However little my Japanese students could understand of me, in lecture or in casual conversation, I could understand still less— that is, nothing—of them, or of any human sounds I heard in Japan. I was paradoxically deaf, or at least uncomprehending; I saw mouths moving but grasped not a thing. I was liberated, relieved of language and consequently of meaning. In the language of literary theorists and structuralists like Barthes, there were no "signifieds," because there was nothing that might, to my ears, signify anything. Such absence had its own charms.

One afternoon in Kyoto, I scheduled an appointment for a shiatsu massage with a Japanese woman, a friend of a friend, married to an American yoga instructor. On the telephone, she tried to give me directions to her house, which I could not quite follow. We started over and opted instead to meet at a French bakery at the foot of a nearby hill on a convenient bus route. We walked up the hill into one of those quiet, private neighborhoods one finds throughout Japan—minutes off the busy thoroughfares and yet a world away. The street looked like something from Palo Alto or the Hollywood Hills, although the residences were smaller. Japan is not a big country, about the size of California, with 130 million people living tightly packed. Because much of the landscape is mountainous, the populace is contained even more closely and vertically into dense urban areas. My masseuse and her husband lived in a narrow three-story apartment in a duplex building. The massage room was at the top of the house. We went up. I lay down. The windows were open; the day was warm and close. I heard ambient noise. Japanese are trained from childhood not to make loud sounds. I said to the woman that if we were in America or the Mediterranean, we'd be hearing the radios and televisions of our neighbors, not to mention their voices discussing the affairs of the day and other mundane matters. We would hear shouting, screaming, expressions of passion. Think of an Italian village in summer. We would know that all the energies and despairs of human life, the comic and the tragic, surrounded us. According to my local contacts, the Japanese allow only dogs to make noises—these they regard as natural—not people, not machines. From two stories above, I could hear the faint, barely audible sounds of three men talking. I couldn't determine the language, English or Japanese or some combination. Their voices blended with the wind, the wind chimes, and the twitter of the birds. The masseuse asked me whether the human sounds were distracting or annoying; if so, she would ask the men to step outside. No, I said. I heard no words, only murmurs and whispers. I could neither understand nor even really hear what they were saying. It was all foreign, because all sotto voce. It was music to my ears. Not a signifier anywhere, just the magic of sound.

From Dallas, my sometime home, to Japan, it was a long but easy nonstop flight. I had traveled halfway around the world and then returned dazed and refreshed to the former Republic of Texas. I came back to what had been my station for four decades. Dallas felt, as it always does on such a return, familiar if not entirely pleasing. Habit has a great deal to recommend it. So does, even more, breaking habits.

I decided to move to Manhattan.

a two-word label: the "synthetic sublime." Like all cities, but with greater speed and force, Manhattan disappears and reappears, constantly remaking itself architecturally and demographically.

In the nineteenth century, English visitors like Dickens and Fanny and Anthony Trollope came to see for themselves what this New York was all about. Their task was never easy. Manhattan has been, until recently, notoriously dangerous, putrid, dirty, and noisy. In 1851, the American diarist George Templeton Strong called it a "whorearchy," with mud and excrement everywhere. Two and a half million pounds of horse manure were deposited every day until the electric trolley, the subway, and finally the automobile gradually put the quadrupeds out of business.

In 1990, Elizabeth Hardwick lamented the status of "our hysterical, battered and battering, pot-holed bankrupt metropolis." Her contemporary Alfred Kazin, who walked the streets in search of inspiration from the writers of the previous century whom he read and loved, found the Upper West Side in the 1970s and 1980s a repository of "every possible color of skin, decrepitude, eccentricity." He did not intend this as praise. To a young person in Manhattan in the new millennium, several decades after Rudolph Giuliani turned Times Square into the family-friendly, semi-Disneyfied entertainment crossroads of the world, it must be hard to envision the graffiti-covered, garbage-strewn, grittier Manhattan that Kazin and Hardwick bemoaned, torched by arson, blighted by disease. Today's aging hipsters look back nostalgically to that New York as a cauldron of creativity where artists could live in cheap bohemian squalor in downtown buildings that have almost all been improved or victimized by condominiumized gentrification. Between 1990 and 2013, crime in Manhattan dropped by an astonishing 90 percent.

White's generalization still holds true, as does the inevitable nostalgia for older times. Manhattan is the magnet. James Weldon Johnson, the African-American writer from Jacksonville, Florida, felt he "was born to be a New Yorker." Harlem gave him nurture.

To him, and countless others, the words of F. Scott Fitzgerald's Nick Carraway, narrator of *The Great Gatsby*, rang and will always ring true. Carraway saw Manhattan from the Queensboro Bridge. Other people have their vantage point on other bridges, a ferry, Hoboken, the Palisades, a car heading south along the Henry Hudson Parkway, or a plane flying into La Guardia with a long view of the city on one side. Or there is the hope or assurance you experience upon entering the inspiring great hall at Grand Central Terminal, with its majestic vaulted ceiling through which light passes. Looking up at the teal blue (or seafoam?) starry astrological dome in the main concourse (thank you, Jacqueline Kennedy Onassis), you feel, like each new arrival, that Manhattan, on the other side of the doors, has become the repository and symbol "in its wild promise of all the mystery and the beauty of the world."

What White did not think of was the appeal of the city as the final destination for people at the other end of the age spectrum. It can be the final destination—"final" in two ways—for the old as well as the young, although probably not all that many of them. Of *us*, I should say, because I count myself among the senior eccentrics. Most Americans with the urge to leave home and to retire elsewhere tend to go where children and grandchildren live, or to flee from the North to the South in search of warmth, easier living conditions, less expensive housing costs, lower taxes. They get rid of their snow shovels. They will never sand their driveways again. Some of us, perhaps throwing fiscal caution to the winds, do the opposite. Moving to New York might mean what Samuel Johnson said about second marriages: it represents the triumph of hope over experience. But if he can afford it, and can tolerate serious downsizing, what could be more hospitable to an ambulatory senior citizen than Gotham?

Retiring to Manhattan is an act of bravery. It also prepares a person for the end. The anonymity of metropolitan life gets you ready for the anonymity of the grave. I find this assessment comforting rather than macabre.

According to the New York Department for the Aging, the population of people over sixty increased by more than 12 percent between 2000 and 2010 and is projected to grow by more than 35 percent by 2030 to 1.84 million people. We can attribute much of the growth to longevity and some to people's reluctance to give up on old ways, habits, and locales. Certain Manhattan neighborhoods have already achieved NORC (naturally occurring retirement community) status.

There is less information about people like me who have come here belatedly, willingly, even enthusiastically.

"Manhattan": when I was a kid I had the sheet music for Rodgers and Hart's song at home in the Philadelphia suburbs. I played it on our piano when I was twelve. I memorized the tune and the words. The Bronx and Staten Island came later. First as a student and then as an adult, I took to Manhattan, not only for what White called "the gift of loneliness, the gift of privacy," but also for their opposites, the gifts of public life, of crowds, the paradox of anonymous company, and the serendipity of street conversations with strangers. The city remains completely indifferent to me, as it is to everyone. It exists, as nature does, without me even when I am part of it. Without doing anything or talking to anyone, a walker on the street participates in the general excitement. Sitting at a Starbucks or an ordinary diner and looking out, you see life itself on the other side of the window. Whatever your opinion of humanity, you have people to bewilder or console you. Years ago *The New York Times* had a feature about a middle-aged man who had lived, a bachelor, in a mountain cabin. He seldom socialized. Finally, he married. After a modest city ceremony, he returned with his new bride to his rural home. Chivalrous, he lifted her up and carried her across the threshold. "Alone at last," he said. "Except for you, of course." In Manhattan, one is always alone, except for everyone else.

I read with curiosity the stories of people, like this newly married woodsman, who decide to leave the city in search of quiet and privacy on a ranch, on a beach, on a mountaintop, or in the country-side. I figure that the final quiet will come soon enough. The grave offers privacy. I also realize that what I want in the last chapters of life is contact with, not separation from, others. "Independent" housing arrangements for seniors always encourage a kind of camaraderie, cheerful and grim in equal measure. My father lived in such a place for five years. Every day the sound of an ambulance called everyone to momentary, breathless attention. Everyone was waiting. They knew the clock was ticking. Seek not to ask for whom the bell tolls.

I had a recent discussion with a colleague who has decided to retire with his wife to a farmhouse in the Dordogne. I asked whether he knew anyone there. No, he said. "Do you speak French?" No. "Are you handy with home repairs?" No. "Do you understand French legal and commercial habits?" Again, a simple American no. I said that his idea of a challenge, an adventure, a source of pleasure, was my idea of a nightmare. He asked what I dreamed of for the next move. I replied immediately that at the end of the road I do not want to be at the end of a road in some rural hideaway, especially where I do not really know the language. I want to be surrounded by everyone I have ever known or at least by people who share my language and customs.

"Let me tell you," he said, "there's nothing like having a farm-house in the South of France to ensure that everyone you have ever known will make a visit."

Perhaps he is right, I thought, but this is not the same thing as daily life in the presence of relatives and old friends and in the midst of everything that will go on without you after you leave it. You can take comfort in the fact of your cosmic insignificance. You are reminded, in the city, of your utter irrelevance to the greater scheme of the universe. Aging means giving up, de-accessioning, and knowing that all worldly achievement, like wealth, counts for little. Urban life makes you feel like a nobody. Paradoxically, it also makes you feel alive.

The automobile had everything—or at least a great deal—to do with my decision to leave Texas. I grew up driving, champing at the bit to get behind the wheel and get out of the house. Like most Americans, I can divide my life into pre-car and post-car chapters. A driver's license marks any teenager's major rite of passage. My sixteenth birthday gave me freedom, in imagination more than actuality. But the promise of such freedom got me through my high school years. I could escape from home, doing or trying to do what adolescents want to. Many of today's college students have false identification cards so they can gain access to local watering holes. I wanted my driver's license only for purposes of movement. Wheels afforded access to more than just what young people crave: the promise of sex in those hot boxes of callow adolescent passion. They took me to museums, theaters, libraries, country ponds, and friends' houses. They extended my geographic, intellectual, and affective radii. I began to see more of the world, especially the parts I could not reach through the Philadelphia bus and subway lines.

As an adult, I think I have resented every hour I have spent driving a car. When buying my last one—"last," I suspect, in both senses—some fourteen years ago, I went out for the requisite test drive with an overly cordial but not very alert salesman. "Tell me, Willard," he asked hopefully, "isn't it fun driving this car?"

I replied quickly, firmly, but without scorn, "Listen very carefully. The words 'drive' and 'fun' do not belong, for me, in the same sentence." This marked the end of our discussion. I know how un-American and unmanly this claim must sound. Unlike most men, I have also never minded asking for directions, from a car or on foot, when I am lost. My ego is intact without my having to feel in control. Driving, especially fast driving, gives people, especially men, authority. It speaks to their testosterone levels. Some women suffer from the same mania. Surrendering a license often represents the last challenge to the independence of any senior citizen. Some go gentle, others kicking, into their car-free existence. If I had infinite wealth, I would have hired a permanent chauffeur decades ago. Imagine: being driven, while spending your time reading, writing, napping, talking, all things you can do on the subway if you are lucky enough to get a seat. New York, especially Manhattan, leads all American cities in its population of carless drivers. Boston and Washington, D.C., come in a distant second and third. It is possible, with great difficulty, to live without an automobile almost anywhere. But it is seldom convenient.

And I know as well that for many people driving gives something that their lives otherwise lack. I chatted with a young colleague who lives in a Dallas suburb, and I asked about his commute: How long does it take to get home in the afternoon? That depends, he said, on when he leaves campus. At three o'clock, he can make the drive in twenty minutes; at four o'clock, it will take more than twice as long. And then the punch line: he prefers the later drive. Why? I should have known: "It's the only time during the day that I have entirely to myself." Family and attendant chores, the children, the lawn, the dog, the soccer practice and the music lessons, tonight's dinner, and the morning's dishes all awaited him at home. The driving hour, undisturbed by anything other than NPR, music, or Books on Tape, was for him alone.

The automobile liberates us. It also isolates us. Walking focuses and expands the mind. Driving closes the mind to everything except driving itself.

Is anything as sad as a parking lot, or even a multistoried city parking garage, with the rows of abandoned cars bereft of life and waiting for their owners to come back and fire them up? The urban scene must accommodate the automobile as hospitably as it accommodates the human population. A parking garage at least has the modest aesthetic advantage of hiding its inhabitants: you can't see its invisible population of pent-up machines. But nothing can be done to soften the vast expanse of an open-air lot paved in asphalt or concrete. The anomie of hundreds of empty cars always conjures up for me thoughts of an urban graveyard, but at least most cemeteries have appropriate landscaping.

Few visible phenomena in the American environment are as dispiriting as these plots for things already symbolically dead, things lying side by side and piled up above rather than beneath the ground. In addition to nature's softening touches, cemeteries have reminders of human life: tombstones are inscribed with names and dates, and even modest literary allusions. No one has ever wandered through a parking lot for solace. It is not a thing of beauty. Off-hours, it is just a forlorn empty space. But in cities like Dallas, parking facilities are essential. A business, restaurant, shop, or gallery without adequate parking will fail. How can customers get to their destination without a car? And once there, where will they put it?

Privacy is necessary to well-being. Insulation or isolation is not. People have talked of the disintegration of city life, and the alienation it creates in urban dwellers, for more than a century. And yet I never feel more alone than in a car or attempting to navigate on foot through suburban Dallas neighborhoods. One Christmas night, I had to walk—my car having been left in the repair shop—to my office a mile away from home to retrieve something I had forgotten but needed to take to a conference the following day. Whatever festivities were taking place at well-stocked tables in the houses of the haute bourgeoisie, I could neither participate in nor even see from outside. In wealthy Dallas neighborhoods, families leave the rooms at the front of their houses open for view. They never draw the curtains. They are proud to show off the parts of the house they seldom use. The real living is done at the back and out of sight. The living room is for display, mostly for the benefit of people driving through the neighborhood.

So when I walked through Highland Park on that Christmas evening, I never saw another living person. Never have I felt so existentially isolated. On the year's major day of celebration, I was alone, actually and spiritually. In Manhattan, one is alone in the crowd.

One is apart from and a part of it. There's always someone else enjoying a solitary walk. A private meal at the diner can lift the spirits. At least it does not dampen them. Whenever I see Edward Hopper's 1942 painting *Nighthawks*, which the artist said represented "the loneliness of a large city," I feel that I have joined the human race, not separated from it. The four figures—one couple side by side, one additional customer, and the serving guy behind the counter—sit or stand in quiet, uncommunicative postures. We see them through a curved plate glass window. Their diner has no sign of an entrance door or even a window that might open. We are cut off from them but can gain solace from their togetherness. This picture does not fill me with sadness. It portrays the possibility for a self-sufficient community in the least likely circumstances. In their locked bubble, these people have one another. Even if they don't know it, we do.

When I was an adolescent always willing and eager to borrow the car for an evening or even an hour, I also knew about the fabled land of Manhattan, ninety miles north of my little Philadelphia suburb. Jean Shepherd broadcast his off-kilter, neurotic, and often insane monologues over WOR; I listened to him from bed on my tiny radio and wondered what kind of people inhabited this land. When I was sixteen, I took the train with three friends, and we spent a weekend in the city. We stayed at a YMCA and a YWCA on West Twenty-Third Street. We rode the subway uptown to visit older friends who'd already made their getaway to college at Barnard and Columbia and, taking the wrong line, had to hike up through Morningside Park to Broadway, only to learn that we might have been mugged en route. Fortune smiles on the innocent: nothing untoward befell us. Off-Broadway shows (Beckett's *Krapp's Last Tape* and Albee's *Zoo Story*) bewildered us but made us feel sophisticated, just as reading *The Waste Land* did. We smugly pretended that anything easy did not count as art. I could not understand a word of Eliot. I had no sympathy for the condition of Krapp, with his tapes and bananas, or for Albee's two men on a Central Park bench, but it did not matter. I worshipped difficulty and opacity. I knew I had to get back to the place where such incomprehensible artistry and the people who must have understood it seemed to thrive, where coffeehouses were filled with bearded or flaxen-haired folksingers who sang their political protests to left-leaning audiences. We were baby suburban beatniks, in search of our kind.

During my college years, I occasionally made the trip in from the country—my first opera at the old Met, concerts at Carnegie Hall, overnight visits with classmates who lived in Brooklyn and Long Island—and felt the city's appeal, its aching beauty, its clamor punctuated by stillness. Driving down the Henry Hudson Parkway to cross the George Washington Bridge for mandatory holiday visits with my family, I gazed, Carraway-like, in wonder at the Palisades on one side of the river and what seemed like magnificent, eternal granite outcroppings on the New York side. The lights, the buildings, and the marvelous city: everything spelled magic if only because I was always looking up, from below, or out, from a distance. Precisely because I was not at home, I felt at home, speeding along at sixty miles per hour. I wanted to be home, here.

Having partially relocated to Manhattan three years ago, I have taken it upon myself to see as much as I can via foot and subway. I bought a pedometer to measure my progress and also to make a comparison between life in Dallas and life in New York City. In Dallas, it turns out I averaged less than two pedestrian miles per day. Most of that involved walking from parking lot to office and back. And, within my university building, for decades I have walked the seventy-eight steps from the back door to my fourth-floor office. Probably four or five times a day. If I took the elevator and omitted the stairs, I'd have racked up even fewer miles. It is easy to understand why many Americans feel an obligation to go to a gym. We must plan to exercise. On an ordinary Manhattan day—running errands, walking along the local streets, doing nothing special or arduous—I average six miles on foot. If I want to be more leisurely and at the same time get more exercise, I can do ten miles without even thinking about it. It is no wonder that obesity rates are lower in Manhattan than elsewhere in the country.

The possibilities for excitement are endless. And I converted my pleasure into a form of work. I persuaded an editor to commission some journalistic pieces from me, the new walker in the city, a twenty-first-century flaneur in the honored tradition of Baudelaire and Walter Benjamin in Paris, or Alfred Kazin and Joseph Mitchell in Manhattan. I would *do* New York. Everyone can. And everyone's experience will be utterly different from everyone else's.

I like New York in June. If you're looking for healthy excitement when the weather is not too oppressive, let me recommend what I did on the second day of summer. I went for a walk, a long walk. With five like-minded pedestrians, all thirty years younger, I did Manhattan from top to toe, starting at 8:30 and ending eleven hours later, with only modest pedal calluses as uncomfortable reminders the morning after.

The plan was easy. Anyone can follow it, or design his or her own variation. We met at the top of Manhattan, the borough, not the island. A geography question: Where is this? If you said Marble Hill, at 230th Street, located officially in the Bronx on the other side of the Harlem River, but actually part of the borough of Manhattan, you get a star. Very few New Yorkers know this.

We were three college English teachers, one librarian, and two social workers. We were two married couples who had come from the Midwest, one single woman from Queens, and I, who counted as a recent, part-time Manhattanite. We gathered outside the 231st Street No. 1 subway station in the golden light of a Saturday morning. The city was waking up. With its undistinguished red and yellow brick buildings, Upper Broadway qualifies as a melting pot, many but not all of whose ingredients are Caribbean and Hispanic. The

Dolce Vita Salon and Day Spa sits beside the office of a Vietnamese chiropractor, the Gold Mine Cafe ("Open 24 Hours"), the Te-Amo Convenience Store, and Keenan's Irish pub ("est. 1961"). Mr. Mc-Goo's Pub is up Broadway a block, and Loeser's Kosher Deli a block down. Such examples of a United Nations of Commerce exist in almost all New York neighborhoods.

Tourists do not come to this part of the city.

We crossed the Broadway Bridge and headed into Inwood, in Manhattan, its tree-shaded streets filled with sedate single-family houses, small, trim apartment buildings, and well-maintained gardens. By 9:20, it was time for our first snack, pastries from the Isham Street Farmers' Market. Then we continued south, past small Orthodox shuls and the Dyckman Street subway station at Fort Tryon Park, where the tower of the Cloisters rises from the treetops.

On Broadway and 181st Street—aka Juan Rodriguez Way here—we saw a sign for the dental offices of Dr. Moshe Glick and his partner Dr. Olga Iglesias, on top of Colorina Shoes and across from the Pagan Driving School. Nearby: a taco truck called La Viagra. (I wonder what happens after you eat one of its specialties.) Moving past Audubon Terrace, we finally entered Manhattan's more familiar precincts. We stopped for early Bloody Marys and eggs Benedict on 125th Street and Broadway. A little after noon, fortified, we resumed.

Greenery beckoned. We headed down quiet Claremont Avenue paralleling the Hudson. Columbia University had mostly emptied out for the summer. The Dalai Lama was doing a gig at Riverside Church. From the back of the hall, I softly sang to myself "Hello, Dalai!" and then we ambled down leafy Riverside Drive, witnessing en route a bicycle accident—fire truck and ambulance on the scene to rescue the hapless victim, who had slammed into an opening car door—and headed east, past the Cathedral of St. John ("the Unfinished") toward the northwest corner of Central Park.

We circled back to Bank Street Book Store on Broadway (last year, it moved down the street to a new location) for some of our group to find souvenirs for their kids. Catty-cornered, on the northeast side, we saw our first real tourists of the day, snapping photographs in front of Tom's Restaurant. Think *Seinfeld*.

Then into Central Park, weaving between sun and shade, between roller-bladers and canines, through the glorious stand of American elms south of Bethesda Fountain and the kayak-crowded lake. At 2:20, we emerged in front of the Plaza, back in the city again.

Even on a summer weekend, midtown Manhattan throbs with people, mostly tourists. The commuters, office workers, and businesspeople have retreated. We pressed west and then south through Sixth Avenue's street vendors hawking all manner of things to eat, drink, and wear, and hit Rattle N Hum, an Irish pub west of Madison Avenue on Thirty-Third Street. Cold, dark, and empty was the place, with European soccer matches on big TV screens. Cold and dark were the beers, even more appreciated.

A movie crew had occupied a dozen square blocks around Madison Avenue in the twenties and thirties, at what expense one could not even begin to calculate. Traffic had halted. "What are they doing?" we asked. It turned out to be a sixty-second chase scene for an upcoming Spider-Man movie, but we heard this through the grapevine, not the closed-lip traffic controllers. A flatbed truck sped by, carrying the (presumably) dead or wounded body of Spider-Man, or a Spider-Man counterfeit.

Our exciting brush with entertainment left us unsettled, so we turned west through Madison Square Park, went past the Flatiron Building, and down Fifth Avenue to Eleventh Street, one of those tasteful residential blocks that virtually whisper: "The West Village: You Really Cannot Afford to Live Here, But You May Dream" and—after pizza slices on Sixth Avenue—meandered to West Street on the Hudson, where we refreshed ourselves briefly (whiskey and pickles) at the Rusty Knot, full of what looked like local hipsters.

Everyone can discover curiosities during a walk like this and have plenty of questions about history, architecture, and culture.

Smart phones have never been more useful or appreciated. What was that abandoned picture hall on Upper Broadway? It's the old United Palace, featured in that morning's *Times*; it opened in 1930, became the church of Reverend Ike in 1969, and is now engaged in a fund-raising campaign to restore its original magic.

And what about this pseudo-Renaissance edifice, sticking out like a giraffe near the lovely West Village Greek Revival row houses we had just walked past? Julian Schnabel's Palazzo Chupi, a work of art to some, a monstrosity to others, an act of narcissism, vandalism, or sheer chutzpah depending on whom you're listening to.

We moved down the Hudson as breezes rose off it. We got glorious views of New Jersey, the Statue of Liberty, and, looming ahead, the as yet unopened World Trade Center. We bypassed the lines for the Memorial site. One of us had a better plan: go to the top floor of the World Center Hotel, sit on the terrace with drink in one hand and camera in the other, and gaze down at the miracles of lower Manhattan.

At 7:30, having peered through the gates of Bowling Green and admired the stately old Custom House, now the National Museum of the American Indian, we reached Battery Park. We stood by the railing for class pictures. A fisherman volunteered to take one of all six of us.

"We just walked here from the Bronx, 19.58 miles according to our iPhone app," I said.

"You did what?" he replied incredulously. "I live up there. I always take the subway. You should try it."

By 8:00, we were relaxing at an outdoor table on Stone Street, with tourists from all over the world and next to young ladies who seemed to have leaped straight from the cast of *Jersey Shore*. The place was raucous, and the beer wonderful. The noisy vulgarity—what on another day might have annoyed me—added the proper populist touch.

I grabbed a No. 2 subway at Wall Street to get home. The evening had turned mild. No matter how you look at it, or where or when, New York is a helluva town. The Bronx is up, the Battery down.

Having done Manhattan, I set my sights on the outer boroughs. My model of a New Yorker and a writer-about-New-York is the late Joseph Mitchell, whose scrupulous, surprising, and deeply felt sketches and stories about his adopted town graced the pages of *The New Yorker* for decades. A typical day for him would begin with a ride—subway or bus—to a far-off destination, chosen at random, where he would alight, walk around, talk to people, and from which he would return. The characters, louche, down on their luck, colorful, sinister, pathetic, and exciting, come alive in his pages, a testimony to the superiority of art to life, or at least to the difference between the two. Mitchell makes you realize how much better it is to read about his urban specimens than to encounter them for yourself. But you can make your own discoveries. Life is where you find it. And if you live in Manhattan, you don't have to go to a foreign country for stimulation. You might consider Brooklyn.

As someone who had just finished an eleven-hour, twenty-mile Manhattan hike from tip to toe, I figured my next touristic step should be off island, or at least on a different island. But Brooklyn has neither top nor bottom. You can't decide to march down an equivalent of Broadway and call it quits. I needed an expert and also, as it turned out, that most embarrassing of New York luxuries, a car.

My guide was the estimable CUNY sociologist William Helmreich, whose recent book *The New York Nobody Knows: Walking 6,000 Miles in the City* is a lively account of his four years of treks (fifteen hundred miles annually) through all five boroughs. Because I had only one day, the auto was a necessity.

Our visit followed a pattern that anyone can adopt and vary: drive to a neighborhood, get out, walk around, talk to people, take notes, then head to the next spot. One morning in mid-July, the good professor met me at the corner of Montrose and Bushwick, where I had decamped from the L train, far from Manhattan glamour. This is East Williamsburg, an edgy industrial transitional neighborhood, the next DUMBO according to my guide. On one side of Maspeth Avenue, in front of a sweet little park, we saw a new seven-story building ("Condominiums with Resort Style Amenities") across from the Greenpoint Renaissance Center shelter for the working homeless.

We drove along Bushwick Avenue through the gritty projects on the corner of Flushing Avenue. Danger and beauty existed side by side. Stately 1870s mansions in disrepair were undergoing renovation. Pocket gardens sprouted between industrial buildings. When we reached Troutman Street, we had arrived at Graffiti Central: large murals, organized by the Bushwick Collective, add lustrous color and design—sometimes garish, sometimes whimsical—to building fronts. Think of a combination of *Mad* magazine, R. Crumb, Paul Klee, Philip Guston, and Keith Haring. Savvy local street artists have turned the neighborhood into an outdoor museum. Admission is free.

And then: Williamsburg's Hasidim in their standard uniforms pouring along Lee Avenue with its men's hat stores and Scarfs for Her tucked between bakeries and fruit stands run by Orthodox Jews, not Koreans. This is not hip Williamsburg but an old-world Orthodox shtetl. One fast-food joint (Café au Lee) advertises *poutine*, the famous, gloppy Canadian dish—French fries topped with cheese curds and mysterious brown gravy—that is probably no more delectable or savory when served kosher. At 125 Heyward Street, the former P.S. 71, a three-story redbrick Victorian building, now the Williamsburg Senior Citizens Participation Center, we looked in on separate classes, Talmud for the men and Torah for the women, and I saw my first (ever!) stand of toilets with mezuzahs over the doors.

With an urbanist's keen eye, Mr. Helmreich noted that you can often judge the safety of the neighborhood by the fact that older houses retain bars on their windows, whereas new ones have none. He also pointed out the Marcy Houses, across Flushing Avenue from the Hasidic community, where the rapper Jay Z grew up. Surprise and delight awaited everywhere. The rapidly gentrifying Bedford-Stuyvesant/Expanded Stuyvesant Heights Historic District, rows of brownstones built between 1870 and 1920, is spiffing itself up block by block. Romanesque, Queen Anne, and Moorish houses, some with elegant stenciling on their exteriors and lovingly tended front gardens, turn Hancock Street into a stately procession of dwellings.

Thirty years ago, you would not have seen a shopwindow poster declaring: "Poop/Pee Free Zone" and saying "Please Respect Your Neighbors and Your Community."

Brooklyn has charms and surprises, but much of it is not exactly pretty. This is not the New York of a nostalgic Woody Allen film. Driving along Kings Highway past Kings Plaza, the borough's largest shopping center, you might be anywhere in modern America. And then you get to Mill Basin, an enclave of single-family houses in a hodgepodge of styles, ranging from modest 1950s split-levels to garish Miami Beach fantasies, the residences of upwardly mobile Russians from Brighton Beach. I imagined an intense reality television show—*The Real Russian Housewives of Brooklyn*—taking place within the ornate marble halls.

From Mill Basin, we drove through Gerritsen Beach, barely visible from the main street, a district of tiny working-class houses surrounded by chain-link fences, a community with American flags, not mezuzahs, everywhere. It's still largely Irish-Catholic, with a modest German and Italian presence in its population. The two neighborhoods are yin and yang. Then off to Bensonhurst, a genuinely exciting cultural stew. The linguistic and mercantile bustle of Eighty-Sixth Street beneath the elevated D train has a mostly Russian and Chinese flavor, with a touch of Spanish, including a Mexican restaurant, Tortillas King. Under a sign in English and Chinese characters, we saw the words "Yummy" in a fortune cookie script and "Teriyaki Grill" in italics, a typographic symbol of the neighborhood's multilingualism and the melting pot of its cuisine.

The Bnei Baruch Kabbalah Education and Research Institute on Eighty-Fifth Street lies a stone's throw from Vstrecha, a fancy Russian restaurant, and down the block from Steve's Playland, one of Mr. Helmreich's earlier serendipitous finds. (You will make your own.) The Playland is a shrine to American popular culture, a monument of kitsch assembled by Steve Campanella. Marilyn Monroe, Superman, Bogie, Elvis, Lucy Ricardo, Betty Boop, Al Capone, and others, in full-size plastic reproduction, surround all sides of the unassuming house at 2056 Eighty-Fifth Street. A tasteful brass plaque in front announces the maker's purpose: "Preserving the Past, Enriching the Present, and Inspiring Hope for the Future." You won't find stuff like this in your standard Michelin guide.

Dyker Heights' mansions between Eleventh and Thirteenth Avenues, the so-called Park Avenue of Bensonhurst, with their pristine landscaping, clipped topiary, and mismatched statuary (and, at Christmas, traffic-stopping light displays), offered a change of taste. Then we drove down Fourth Avenue into Gowanus, where we stopped on Eighth Street for a visit to one of Mr. Helmreich's other urban discoveries.

A plate glass window at No. 180½ announced—with beautiful lettering on a building devoid of other signs of commerce—"P. de Rosa Grocery," with Schaefer and Rheingold beer signs beneath. The main entrance to the house is next door, at No. 180. What was this?

If you see something, ask something: that's the key to becoming an urban sociologist. On an earlier trek, Mr. Helmreich had met Mr. de Rosa's grandson, who gave him the skinny. Paolo de Rosa came to Brooklyn at the turn of the last century and opened his little market, which closed in 1972. His son and now his grandson have kept the original plate glass intact as a gesture of respect to the Sicilian *nonno*.

Paul de Rosa and his wife, Doris, came outside. I asked about an appealing nineteenth-century frame house across the street, nestled between two brownstones. "That was the original farmhouse here," Mr. de Rosa said. It's now the residence of Steve Hindy, the owner of Brooklyn Brewery. Who knew? The moral: Ask and you shall learn.

The day was ending. By the time I returned to the Upper West Side, I had walked only nine miles but traveled much farther. The drive out of Gowanus took me through the more fabled parts of a cool person's Brooklyn: Carroll Gardens (you know gentrification has occurred when you see restaurants with umbrellas over outdoor tables), Cobble Hill, Boerum Hill, and Park Slope. Mr. Helmreich deposited me at Pratt Institute's quiet, leafy campus. Walking back to the subway, I saw that I was surrounded by young white people, all of them wearing black.

I knew that Manhattan was right around the corner. And having ventured off island, I also decided that I had to do the other three boroughs, the ones less visited. And I did.

Everyone knows the real reason to exercise is to give you license to eat more. If you like food but are not blessed with a high metabolism, there is an easy formula for happiness: Burn calories in order to consume more calories. With this formula in mind, I took it upon myself to walk and eat my way for the better part of a summer day through Queens, New York's most ethnically, linguistically, and culinarily diverse borough. You cannot do it all. My eight-hour, twelve-mile multicultural eating binge omitted a lot of cuisines (Greek, Afghani, Indian, Bosnian, and Malaysian, as well as the more obscure ones) and territory, especially glamorous enclaves like Kew Gardens and Douglaston.

With two foodie companions, the first a distinguished journalist and food writer, the second a young editor living in this outer borough, I crossed the Queensboro Bridge (*The Great Gatsby* in reverse!)—with its beautiful views, deafening car noise, and dangerous bicyclists—and soon, on our right side, we could see the Steinway Storage Warehouse and the Hotel Z, symbols of the old and the new Queens, face off. We arrived at Queens Plaza. By eleven o'clock, away from racket and grit, we had reached a quiet residential neighborhood on Skillman Avenue, with sturdy six-story red-brick apartment complexes and front gardens.

At Forty-Third Street, Skillman Avenue becomes known as Lewis Mumford Way, in honor of the twentieth-century American man of letters who lauded the enclave of Sunnyside Gardens, that planned working-class community on quiet, tree-shaded streets, with row and semidetached houses, and one of only two private parks—Manhattan's Gramercy is the other, more famous one—in the city. At 11:30, famished, we stopped for our first, and only European, food: mouthwatering croissants and brioches at the neighborhood La Marjolaine Bakery.

Then the real urban adventure began.

Roosevelt Avenue, under the elevated No. 7 line, took us away from Woodside, a former Irish area (Donovan's Pub and the Stop Inn bear the evidence), now largely Filipino. Diversity, that much overused term, is in full view: the V&V Italian Bakery, advertising "Fresh Irish Soda Bread," stands across from La Fina Colombian Bakery and Restaurant, and close to Salvadoran and Ecuadoran eateries. At El Nuevo Izalco Restaurant, aka La Casa de las Pupusas, we stopped for a trio of the eponymous light corn pancakes stuffed, individually, with pork, cheese, and beans. We planned, but forgot, to top these off with some fig ice cream from next door.

By Seventieth Street, it's still Filipino (stores advertising balikbayan boxes, for sending gifts), but finding the New York Cho Dae Church (Presbyterian) across the street from the Jackson Heights Islamic Center and Mosque, and around the corner from the Greek Orthodox Church of SS Constantine and Helen, I suddenly remembered that the United Nations' first home was appropriately here in Queens.

The quest continued. At 12:45, hungry once more, we alighted at the Himalayan Yak Restaurant for—what else?—steamed yak dumplings; goat Bhutan (intestine, liver, heart, and stomach, stir-fried with butter, green chilies, onion, tomatoes, and Nepalese herbs, the whole dish crackling like pork rinds, with tripe the dominant flavor); and *laphing*—that's sliced mung bean jelly to you—a slithery concoction flavored with peppers, chili, and soy sauce.

The blocks through Corona are Hispanic all the way. The neighborhood has a few outliers like the anomalous Martiniello's Pizzeria; otherwise it is Dominican, Guatemalan, Ecuadoran, Peruvian. I wanted to sample the wares of at least one food truck, so at 104th and Roosevelt we stopped, circa 2:15, at a taqueria, where we made our only mistake. In addition to the simpler steak and chicken tacos, we opted for *oreja* (ear), which my more sophisticated co-travelers found blander and more gelatinous than other ears they had eaten in, for example, Chinese restaurants. Chalk it up to experience. I had never had an ear before. I don't think I'll eat a second one.

On we soldiered: under Grand Central Parkway, over the Van Wyck, past Citi Field and the automobile graveyards at Willets Point that look like a dangerous scene out of Dante's *Inferno* or *The Waste Land*. Finally, we hit Flushing. At Main Street and Roosevelt Boulevard, you have reached an Asian epicenter (including, in full view of families strolling and shopping with children in tow, Romantic House Adult Store), with fruit stands selling ripe cherries for five dollars a pound and blueberries for one dollar a pint, one-third their Manhattan prices.

We descended a flight of stairs at Main Street's Golden Shopping Mall: you find eight separate but largely indistinguishable kitchens churning out individual delicacies, with plenty of authenticity but neither glamour nor pretense, in a grungy basement. We had settled on Xi'an Famous Foods, where we chowed down on Liang-Pi cold-skin noodles, which were inscrutably warm, and buckwheat cold noodles, gelatinous, smooth, spicy, and tender all at once.

In Flushing, you hear a babel of languages. You see odd juxtapositions. Anomalous cultural melting-pot partnerships abound: the historic St. George's Episcopal Church faces a poster for the law firm of Sackstein Sackstein and Lee (two Jewish fellows and one Korean) on Main Street.

We backtracked, turning right on Northern Boulevard to see Flushing's historic main square. The shingle-style Friends' Meeting House (1694), New York's oldest house of worship in continuous use (and the second oldest in the nation), offered a sober note of austerity to balance a day of self-indulgent sensuality.

This was only our penultimate stop. Almost next door to the Quakers, we finished our day in Queens at Hunan House. We decided against fragrant pig ears, numbed and spicy duck neck, and sautéed spicy fish stomach, in favor of two appetizers, stinky bean curd (fermented in vinegar, and not so easy to love) and wood ear in vinegar sauce (wild mushrooms with plenty of garlic), plus a conventional but spicy sautéed green pepper with pork.

By six o'clock, it was time to stop. At 7:30, I had one final nosh, at home: the dragon fruit I had bought at a Chinese market. It looked like a cross between an artichoke and a big, festive red hand grenade. Cut it open and you find sweet, tender meat. Think kiwi. It goes down nicely with a light French rosé.

By comparison to Manhattan, Brooklyn, and Queens, my solo trips to the Bronx (not the real Bronx but the leafy, quasi-suburban Riverdale section, perched along the Hudson and offering spectacular views of Manhattan to the south) and the last, on Halloween, to Staten Island (also with the help of a car) were less exotic. The journey, not the arrival, matters. And even quiet Riverdale has its appeal, especially to someone who grew up, as most of us do, in a suburb and may want to get a nostalgic reminder of his childhood. If one likes subways, buses, even a ferry—and the Staten Island Ferry, offering the most expansive, sublime views of Manhattan and its harbor, charges no fare—then the excitement of going to a place, getting out, walking around, and coming home twelve hours later has all the magic of a trip abroad without the accompanying hassle of airports, security guards, long lines, and airplane turbulence. One can have an urban adventure in any city. Even a walk around the block, anywhere, to someone with attentive eyes and ears, can offer new and surprising stimulation, but nothing beats New York for the sheer variety of landscape, cityscape, and urban population.

My grandmother used to say, "You'll find nice people everywhere." By that she meant, mostly, Jews. No matter where you are or whom you are counting, this is a truth universally acknowledged. Until recently, common wisdom has held that New Yorkers, like Parisians, are snooty, rude, or too busy to be approachable. Walking with too much speed and determination, they cannot be stopped. Southern friendliness, with its often unctuous, slow, and treacly charm, gets high marks. I have never found the stereotypes accurate. Parisians have always met my efforts at schoolboy French with nothing worse than patient amusement, never scorn. Smiling always helps in foreign countries. And down-home Texans and other south-of-the-Potomac residents might as easily kill you with whispered insults when you have left the room as greet you with their buttery "How ya doin'?" and "Bless your heart" welcomes. People on the streets of Manhattan, especially in the post–Rudy Giuliani period, engage willingly in conversation when one makes an appropriate opening gambit. Southern molasses sweetness is no less a convention than sharp, tangy New York vinegar.

Manhattan is a small village, or an accumulation of many small villages. An apartment building is a community. A block is a federation of constituent communities. The city replicates itself every five blocks or so. The neighborhood market, barbershop, shoe repair shops, dry cleaners, liquor store, all become part of one's daily or weekly drill. You make friends in the shops. There's a famous urban fable, to which Italians would put the label "Se non è vero, è ben trovato" (If it's not true, it ought to be). This is the kind of thing you see written up in the columns of *The New York Times'* Metropolitan Diary and *The New Yorker's* Talk of the Town. One fall afternoon, at Manhattan's redoubtable Fairway Market on Broadway at Seventy-Fourth Street, filled with dangerous, cart-pushing ladies of a certain age, all of whom are in hard-edged pursuit of a mission, the reporter sees and overhears a woman examining the string beans. Speaking perhaps only to herself, she is entranced by the quality of the produce: "Such beans, I've never seen such gorgeous beans." Picking over them individually, she then turns to him and repeats her excitement: "Have you ever seen such beans? You can't get green beans like these where I live."

Thinking that perhaps she has come from the Bronx, New Jersey, or even farther away, he politely asks, "Where are you from, madam?"

"I'm from Eighty-Fifth Street."

Even at the enormous Williams-Sonoma at the Time Warner Center in Columbus Circle that looks more like a Dallas mall, vertical rather than horizontal, than a uniquely New York habitat, I spent thirty minutes chatting with a salesperson who turned out to be an opera singer just back from her summer at a singing institute in Verona. "So what's your *Fach?*" I asked. That stopped her. She was impressed that I knew the German word for a singer's temperament as well as her range. (She is a soubrette, as it turned out.) And then the conversation went further: she had majored in chemistry in college before changing tracks and pursuing a musical career. I totally ignored the place mats I was supposed to be buying. I'm sure I'll never see this woman again. I don't remember her face, but I won't forget our conversation. Chance encounters like this can brighten the day: offering travel instructions in German to a pair of older tourists looking for Jazz at Lincoln Center, or talking in Italian to sweat-drenched Romans in town for the New York City Marathon who wondered where they might find the subway to get them back downtown. A whole series of these meetings is like the grace notes in a musical score: inessential but sweeter for their uselessness.

Or, to change the metaphor, these trivial moments are like pieces of punctuation in a writer's paragraphs: they create pauses, continuities, hesitations, and momentary stopping points. Through them we ask questions or get answers to earlier questions. They provoke exclamations of wonder and good humor. A semicolon joins two independent clauses; a chat brings together two independent people who would otherwise have remained separate. Such punctuation stabilizes the rhythm of each day's syntax.

Random meetings are, like four-minute twirls around a dance floor with different partners, little love affairs without consequences. In a review of books about walking, the *New Yorker* writer Adam Gopnik recently reminisced about the long Sunday walks he took in the 1980s. He was new to the city, just out of graduate school. He would tramp through lower Manhattan, before Tribeca became arrogantly gentrified. He felt the same liberation experienced half a century earlier by Alfred Kazin. Gopnik deliciously calls it "the vague excitement of unearned ease." Thirty years later, SoHo and the rest of Manhattan are different. But so is Adam Gopnik. He makes the easily refutable claim "Walking for pleasure is an occupation of the young. Only a few older people of great vitality walk long in cities."

I could not disagree more. How wrong he is. I am an older person of ordinary vitality. My walks are intended less to observe architecture and civic beauty—Gopnik's main subjects of attention—than to watch the other aspects of life, the flora and fauna, the flowers blooming, the ginkgoes dropping their yellow leaves all at once on a single fall night, the earnest dog walkers with their sniffing canine companions, and especially the entire human species. Walks engage the eye; they promote meditation; they calm and excite simultaneously. A real urban *Spaziergang*, a stroll, resembles a work of art, in Immanuel Kant's rightly epigrammatic definition: it exhibits *Zwecklichkeit ohne Zweck*, purposefulness without purpose. You do not know where you are going until you think it over afterward, when you consider where you have gone. And you do not care. Walks also offer the thrill of surprise. They are a mundane species of performance art. Everyone contributes. Everyone is part of the spectacle.

You run into everyone. Sometimes you bump into old friends, and occasionally you see people you might have heard of, even celebrities. Peripatetic, I met Dante and Plato on the same July day. The former, an African-American security guard at my apartment building, seemed to be sleeping standing up when I stopped in front of him. With a change of costume, this man with ramrod posture could have been an English Beefeater at Buckingham Palace. He might also have been unconscious. With eyes closed, he said, "I can see you looking at me. I am not asleep." Then he opened his eyes. We chatted. It turned out he was not dozing but meditating to ward off a bad migraine he felt coming on. His badge identified him. He was, however, clearly not Italian. "Were you named for the poet?" I asked, half joking. "Sure thing. Awesome dude. Great man," he replied. Was he, too, joking? I could not tell. I did not care.

Hours later in Riverside Park, out for a postprandial stroll, I met Plato. Plato was a parrot, leashed and walking on a garden rail, his owner standing nearby. She was an Upper West Sider straight from central casting: an artsy woman of a certain age, wearing an embroidered Mexican folk blouse, turquoise brooches, silver bracelets, and dangling earrings. Her hair, graying and unruly, was piled high in a bun. Everyone in this section of the park seemed to know her; everyone also knew Plato, who, she said, has about one hundred words. He perched for photographs on my arm. He might have shared some conversation with me, but a passing friend warned his owner that she had spotted a resident hawk circling around, so the lady scooped Plato up and went back home to the small apartment they share with two cats. One beatnik, one bird, two cats: what a ménage, I thought. Strolling back to my place, I counted my little blessings: first, the serendipity of encounter, and second, the cutting short of something that could have gone on too long. Would Plato, his owner, and I have talked longer and achieved deeper intimacies? None of us will ever know.

Dallas, my residence for more than half my life, has had a kind of earned familiarity, the comfort that accompanies habit, but not unearned ease. Manhattan, my residence for a concluding chapter or two, will always generate the excitement of anonymity. It makes me feel I belong there precisely because I do not.

Walt Whitman, quintessential Manhattan walker, described his urban support and comfort as "the impalpable sustenance of me from all things, at all hours of the day." He strikes the right, paradoxical note. Wandering through the city at all hours produces an impalpability that nevertheless is grounded in the body, in the life of everything and everyone around him that gives him physical and more than physical sustenance:

> The simple, compact, well-join'd scheme, myself disinte-
>   grated, every one disintegrated yet part of the scheme,
> The similitudes of the past and those of the future,

> The glories strung like beads on my smallest sights and
>   hearings, on the walk in the street and the passage over
>   the river,
> The current rushing so swiftly and swimming with me
>   far away,
> The others that are to follow me, the ties between me
>   and them,
> The certainty of others, the life, love, sight, hearing of
>   others.
>   ("Crossing Brooklyn Ferry")

Belonging and "disintegrated" simultaneously, Whitman ambles around, both in and out of his wandering game. He observes a scene, in the double sense of that verb: he watches it from without, and he performs a ritual, in this case the ritual of walking with and in the crowd. It is the ritual that all city dwellers, especially New Yorkers, understand and relish. From such scenes, rituals, and walks, Whitman amassed *Leaves of Grass*, the book that changed American literature. Walking gave Whitman the "sights and hearings" that he folded into his poetry. Reading that poetry, indeed reading any book, can sustain a walker like me when he then steps indoors, away from the crowd, and into the solitude of the library.

BOOKS

Of making many books there is no end, and much study is a weariness of the flesh.

—ECCLESIASTES

Manhattan, which always changes, always remains the same. We might say the same thing about books, and about reading. However one's reading habits develop and alter through time, books can stay permanent fixtures in our lives, companions to return to. We have chance encounters with some of them; we make repeat visits to others. Some last forever, and others we banish to charity sales, whether or not we have forgotten their contents. Even those we reread repeatedly change as well as stay the same. The book we read at twenty is not the same one we read again at sixty. Just as the faces we see in the city, Pound's "petals on a wet, black bough," appear and vanish quickly, individual books come and go. Even saying "come and go" metaphorically suggests the connections between moving one's feet through the city and moving one's eyes over pages of black print. Reading books continues, an unending activity, especially for those who got hooked early. At least it has remained permanent for me.

Surely Stéphane Mallarmé was thinking of Ecclesiastes when he began his early poem "Brise marine" ("Sea Breeze") with a similar sense of wearied frustration: "La chair est triste, hélas! et j'ai lu tous les livres." The flesh and the spirit have both become weakened; the promise of books to be read, or to be written, begins to look inadequate or unappealing. Study, endless reading, and plodding attempts to write all result in sadness, not exultation. Even if not deliberately echoing the Old Testament, Mallarmé was expressing the desperation of writers in all languages and cultures. Bound by compulsion, desire, and pride, authors balance their lives between the poles of hope and disappointment.

So do readers. I began as one. Many people do. I then proceeded to write. Most people do not go that far. For every book, essay, review, or piece of journalism I have written, I have read thousands of pages more. In high school, I read, and then took as a personal motto, Francis Bacon's coolly authoritative and precise epigram (in the essay "Of Studies") "Reading maketh a full man; conference a ready man; and writing an exact man." I have spent a lifetime reading, conferring—mostly in classrooms—and writing. Reading came first; the other activities followed. There was a time before I wrote, but I cannot quite remember when. I fiddled with words in print in first and second grades. And I certainly cannot remember the still earlier time when I did not read. Most obsessive readers begin young and are blissfully ignorant, until later, of why they do what they do.

Reading has a history. Scholars like Sven Birkerts and Alberto Manguel have detailed for us the changes in reading as a cultural practice, from the days when most people had to be read to, to the modern habit of silent, individual reading. What about the reading of a person who has reached senior status: How has it changed over the decades? How can a lifelong reader measure the course of his own history? Like any attempt at self-analysis, tracking these changes means taking a backward look and a recovery of facets of the person one used to be, and still is, if only in part. Our tastes and customs alter as we age, as both body and mind undergo time's often not so subtle depredations. "Progress" is hardly the right word; we adjust and adapt for better or worse, and the reader we were at seven or seventeen is not the reader we are at seventy. The eyes require help—stronger glasses, more light, larger print—and the mind might have lost its own *Sitzfleisch*, the simple ability to sit still and concentrate. Even people with sturdy patience succumb, in the age of the tweet, to modest doses of attention deficit disorder. Focus, both mental and physical, may become difficult to maintain. We must work more strenuously at what once seemed easy, even effortless. We persevere, because reading still brings information, stimulation, and solace. It is the first and the ultimate pleasure.

Of one's plans and aspirations, one begins to eliminate items from the lists one made in youth. Things formerly aspired to are now erased as the unrealizable dreams of a different person. I won't learn Mandarin; I probably will not even get to China; I will never master the Argentine tango; I certainly will not swim the Channel. And I know that there are plenty of books I am not going to read, things I have scratched off the to-do sheet. Schopenhauer, Kant's first and second *Critiques*, all of Ezra Pound's *Cantos*, Nabokov's *Ada*, Melville's *Pierre; or, The Ambiguities*. They all elicit an unambiguous "I'd rather not." Time's passing requires that we make choices, positive and negative.

Yeats said, hopefully, "Bodily decrepitude is wisdom." A sentient, honest person will register how the mind declines along with the body. When I was a college senior, I read all of *À la recherche du temps perdu*, although with more than an occasional glance at the Scott Moncrieff translation, for an independent study in Proust. Today the English version alone presents what look like insurmountable challenges. Back in my salad days, right before Proust, I did a seminar in Henry James. Four eager English majors sat at the feet of a brilliant assistant professor, in his house, every Monday evening for four hours. The drill: one novel a week, including the daunting last masterpieces. Anyone who teaches today's college students will confirm that you cannot expect a twenty-year-old to read *The Golden Bowl* in a week and come away understanding anything at all. Looking back, I know that I must have managed only the skimpiest comprehension, bullying my way through the Master's baroque, recondite late style, metaphorically chopping through the underbrush of his inviolable syntax with a machete, my eyes glazing over. Today's college students have more on their plates and in their schedules than I ever did. Some college professors have thrown up their hands and accepted the new realities; they assign only parts of books, selections from Melville, juicy chunks of Homer. Education has returned to the principle of exposing students to the greatest moments, the biggest hits, the most purple passages. It's as though the *Reader's Digest Condensed Books* have come back to life.

Half a century ago, high schools and universities provided space and time for expansive leisureliness, openness, and wandering by the way. One cannot read *Middlemarch* or *Moby-Dick* unless one has unencumbered hours to lose oneself in the text. I have the time today. But rereading *The Wings of the Dove* would challenge me as much as it would any undergraduate with a surgically attached mobile phone and constant buzzing distractions from outside. The senior mind wanders. I have resisted Twitter, but I know as well that brevity has a lot to do with changes in reading habits. Two kinds of brevity: shorter books and shorter periods of time in which to read them.

For purposes of travel, especially on vacation, I always carry with me one big book, a loose and baggy monster, usually a novel that I can tuck into at night, on the plane, or in random moments of leisure, waiting for a friend or a bus. I want something I can open and close and be assured of finishing within two or three weeks. If I have to keep at it for much longer, I risk forgetting the start of the book as I heave toward its end. I don't have the memory required to retain plot details and dialogue, not to mention echoes and repetitions, themes and variations, all the things an English teacher dazzles his students with.

Not having a perfect memory, however, has many wonderful rewards. One can reread books one read years before with the delicious double pleasure of coming upon some things as if for the first time—"What a beautiful sentence," "Yes, she delves wisely into the human heart," "I can't believe this man said that"—and experiencing others with a shock of recognition. "Oh, I remember this part" vies with "I can't wait to see what happens next."

Rereading books from youth or even a later period has another advantage as well. You know that you have guaranteed yourself a good return on your investment. With age, one is more aware of time slipping away as well as accumulating. What does one read? When a friend makes a recommendation, or a review prompts your interest and you decide to make an outlay of time or even money, how long do you give yourself to be drawn in, captured, and lost in your indulgence? One chapter? Ten pages? A hundred? Three hours? Ever hopeful, you may say to yourself, "This is unfolding pretty slowly. The author is setting the stage carefully, engaging our attention by focusing on small details that will become more important when she discloses secrets later." How much later?

Reading runs its own risks, and choosing a book is like sitting down at the gaming tables. When will you strike it rich? Reach the payoff? On the next page? If you are smart, you may decide to cut your losses at a certain point and shut the book. (If you have bought an expensive ticket for a play or concert and find the experience painful or tedious, do you stick around after the intermission, on the theory that you've paid for the seat so you might as well get your money's worth? Or do you decide that time is more valuable than money and head for the exit and then an earlier bedtime?)

The book bores you; it does not engage you; it has inspired nothing other than irritation, tedium, even sleep. It is now time to look elsewhere.

In youth, I read promiscuously. With age, one loses that kind of energy. One makes choices. With an old favorite (here please insert your own selection: mine include Austen, Cather, Dickens, George Eliot, Forster, Woolf), you know you won't go wrong. I reread *Pride and Prejudice* or *Persuasion* every few years. I must have read *Mrs. Dalloway* so many times—including once sitting on the floor of a university library when I had several hours to spare—that I have virtually memorized it as if it were a lyric poem. I have reread both *Moby-Dick* and *Middlemarch* within the past decade, and each took up the better part of a year. I know that *David Copperfield*, which enchanted me in seventh grade, will enchant me still. An essay by Montaigne: anywhere, anytime.

As a habit, reading takes hold early and lasts as long as eyesight does. Or even beyond: many former readers, now sight-impaired, rely on audiobooks, and some of them insist on using the verb "read" to describe what they do while listening. Readers tend to be dreamy and escapist, imagining other worlds, other selves. Some are skimmers; some are divers. Some stick to the surface, darting from item to item like my promiscuous adolescent self; others like to submerge themselves, reading deeply rather than widely, like an adult happily committed to a partner or spouse. They want mastery; if one work of a writer seduces them, they look forward to more of the same. These people—maybe obsessives, maybe just intellectuals—wish to learn as much as possible about a given subject or author. The late Guy Davenport hated the word "erudite" but had as encyclopedic a mind and a reading history as one might imagine. He was the kind of voracious lifetime reader, rare even in the mid-twentieth century, who is a member of an endangered species today. Mark Scroggins describes visits to his former mentor in Lexington, Kentucky, the two friends facing each other in easy chairs, discussing what they have been reading: "The canonical went without saying—he knew his Shakespeare, his Dickens, his Shelley and Coleridge. He had worked his way through all thirty-nine volumes of Ruskin's works, and had spent a summer with Sir Walter Scott's twenty-seven Waverley novels. One time he lamented that he might not get around to reading all of Bulwer-Lytton."

I dare anyone to find more than a handful of people, even or especially literary academics, most of whom have buried themselves in the minutiae of their subspecialties, of whom one might say, "The canonical went without saying."

Guy Davenport neither drove a car nor owned a television. Like Larry McMurtry, reputed to have known the whereabouts of everything in his now partly depleted sprawling stores in Archer City, Texas, he was first and foremost a man of the book. McMurtry—a professional bookman as well as a reader and writer—has called hanging around used bookstores the greatest part of his education. The critic Stanley Edgar Hyman and his wife, the novelist Shirley Jackson, inhabited a ramshackle frame house in North Bennington, Vermont, every nook overflowing with books, every room stocked floor to ceiling. Both the critic and the novelist could say where anything was: "the bookcase at the top of the stairs, second shelf from the bottom, on the left-hand side," or words to that effect, according to generations of admiring colleagues and students. A life devoted to, and defined by, literature, by reading as the all-consuming passion, is harder to imagine in the twenty-first century. C. K. Stead, New Zealand's preeminent man of letters, titled a 2008 selection of essays and reviews *Book Self: The Reader as Writer and the Writer as Critic.* Stead is himself a poet, novelist, and essayist. In other words, not only a man of the book but a man who considers his "self" to be a book, or to be made of books. Think of other encyclopedic readers: the late Canadian scholar Northrop Frye, who could "anatomize" and categorize imaginative and critical literature because of his wide-ranging expertise; or the Stanford professor Franco Moretti, a skimmer rather than a diver, who prefers what he calls "distant" reading to close reading in order to take long views of his specimens; or the anomalous critic Harold Bloom, whose prodigious memory makes him a one-man Google. Giants of reading are never snobs; they take to everything, traveling in the realms of tin and brass as well as silver and gold. Book men and women are rare birds, but they seldom flock together. Each moves idiosyncratically, sensitive only to the demands of instinct and curiosity.

We ordinary or "common"—the term beloved of Dr. Johnson—readers, even academics like me, often lack the stamina or retentive powers to emulate let alone compete with the geniuses of total recall. But we, too, wander at will among literary types, genres, and quality. Virginia Woolf had it only partly right in the summary distinction from her 1916 essay "Hours in a Library": "Let us begin by clearing up the old confusion between the man who loves learning and the man who loves reading, and point out that there is no connection whatever between the two." Although I understand what she means, many of us love both.

From the sublime to the mundane, the ennobling to the trashy, a genuine reader will pick up anything in sight, often regardless of style or substance, rather than do something else. When trapped, he'll aim for a matchbook cover. Anything will serve. Reading inspires, amuses, and instills more than wisdom or even information. In the age of instant reference, when facts (that may turn out to be factoids, fictions, or falsehoods) are always available with a flick or click of the finger and a trip to the Internet, we have less need to perform heroic mnemonic acts. And surfing is not the same as browsing, at least for people of a certain age who can recall scanning library or bookstore shelves, looking for something and then finding more interesting the books that stood next to it. Children who catch the reading bug early know all too well the power and pleasure that arise from having mastered first one's letters, then the words, the sentences, and the meanings discovered on the printed page. That combination, rather than information seeking, keeps them going into adulthood.

The question of what one reads, and how reading habits change with age, inevitably inspires a complementary one: What does one think about, and do with, the physical books themselves? Many of us remember beloved books, the dog-eared copies that were the literary equivalent of the favorite panda, rabbit, teddy bear, or blanket we carried around until it finally deteriorated after too many insults or washings. As we became more serious, we began accumulating, at first unconsciously and then with greater deliberation, our own collections. For people who think of libraries as safe havens, islands of calm in the sea of life's storms, the easiest way to propitiate the gods of chaos is to buy or build real bookshelves, which act as metaphorical protective bulwarks, capable of withstanding the assaults of surly siblings, unsympathetic or uninterested parents, and then other bullies and unpleasant data from the external world. The bedroom, the library, or—as in the case of Hyman and Jackson—the entire house becomes a literary fortress.

What happens when you must dismantle the fortress? When you have to move? Everyone over a certain age has experienced at least one version of the dreaded experience. You have built student bookshelves from boards and cinder blocks or purchased cheap bookcases from IKEA. You have filled rooms with books left over from college courses, which you have never opened again but think you might, and other books bought for pleasure, which you might have reread and annotated. You have decorated a room, an apartment, a whole house, with books. You now find that it is time to leave it behind or to take it all with you. You have changed jobs, sold a house, had a divorce. You put everything into boxes. You carry the boxes—if you are poor or unlucky—down and then up stairs. You replace them on other shelves in your new digs.

How many times can one do this? At least wedding gifts you

have never opened can rest comfortably in the attic, garage, or basement and await the moving men when you must relocate. Or you can drive them directly to Goodwill. They do not take up interior domestic space that might be filled to better purpose. Getting rid of things has advantages. Some years back, I wrote a book called *Seven Pleasures*. I think of it as my book of gerunds: Reading, Walking, Looking, Dancing, Listening, Swimming, and Writing. When I was only a little younger, I might have added "Accessorizing" to the mix. Now I would replace that with "De-accessioning," the pleasure that leads to the beauties of spareness and simplicity.

At the age of forty, I sold a house and put all my worldly goods in storage for the year I left town. I knew that I would purchase, and move into, a smaller place when I returned. I had my big chance to clean, to clear, to cull. How to proceed? I began removing the books from the shelves, individually and lovingly; a gentle patina of dust covered all of them, but each one brought back memories or told a story about where I read it and why, a story about who I was when I read it. How can you sell your children?

Abstruse philosophy turned out to have a respectable practical value: Hegel helped to break the ice. Who would have thought it? I opened my paperback copy of his *Phenomenology*, unregarded for more than twenty years. The print was—still—small, and the pages had yellowed. The spine had lost its glue. I realized that I would never read or need this book again and that if by some bizarre chance I had to reread Hegel, I could always find a better copy in the university library. Borrow books, for free! As a college student, I insisted on ownership; as a wiser adult, I understood that ownership, like all pretenses to control, is itself both a burden and an illusion. Into a cardboard box went Hegel's *Phenomenology*. Then the floodgates opened. More volumes followed Hegel into the bins slated for resale. I have never missed one of them. And I still have not reread Hegel.

In 2005, I chatted with the late poet Mark Strand about a move he was making from Chicago to New York. He had taken a position at Columbia with a lease on an apartment much smaller than his previous one. I asked how he had pared down belongings, especially books. "Willard," the seventy-year-old sage replied, "you don't really need more than a hundred books." A young person, especially a serious reader with a bibliophile's acquisitive instincts, will not recognize the truth of Strand's wise remark. An older person will. "Reason not the need," urged King Lear, who should have known better. In the digital age, all that recommends books as material objects, unless you are a scholar with specific or arcane demands, is their aesthetic appeal, their manifestation of cultural capital, or their marginalia, reminders of your former self. In London and elsewhere, I have seen antiques shops that sell books by the meter or yard, often merely fake cardboard boxes with genuine leather spines turned out, which will give the appearance of a gentleman's library. Books used to furnish rooms. Now the entertainment center has replaced both the library and the hearth. It symbolizes power, pleasure, connection, and community. And, as I have noticed, only older houses and apartments have anything resembling a library. It has gone the way of the working fireplace.

If a person is what he reads as well as what he eats, you can take his measure by a quick look at his nightstand. Not the coffee table with its picture books, its ornamental art and collections of photography, and not even the bookshelves, which bear witness to collecting and to work untouched in years. Like the medicine cabinet and the refrigerator, the bed stand bears witness to daily habits or, more precisely, nocturnal ones. It is an intimate, revelatory piece of furniture. A person creeps into bed and either fuels or at least occupies himself as he escapes from the world and work. He begins an inner journey, one that may first keep him up and then knock him out.

Here is my latest inventory: Sarah Ruden's lively verse translation of the *Aeneid*; Jonathan Galassi's bilingual version of the *Canti* of Giacomo Leopardi; the correspondence of Elizabeth Bishop and Robert Lowell; art criticism by Jed Perl and music criticism by Alex Ross; Helen Vendler on the poems of Emily Dickinson; a cheap paperback detective novel by Erle Stanley Gardner presented to me by a Perry Mason fan. All of them have sat piled up for about a year. I read, as I move, more slowly at night. I dip in at random. I rearrange the books in their several piles. Supine, I do not stay awake for more than thirty minutes in bed. I try to make my reading serious, but at my age I am fighting a losing battle. Sleep always wins, and sooner now than it used to, when I propped myself up in bed at summer camp, a flashlight under the covers, engaging in an activity both stimulating and forbidden after we were supposed to shut down for the night. These days, I am usually out before the lights are.

My bedside books lack long, and usually any, works of fiction. None approaches bestseller status; none is from this year. Most tellingly, they are all things that can be read, even poked through, nonsequentially. Virgil tells a story, of course, but I have read the *Aeneid* so many times, in so many versions, that I can open his epic of arms and men, and women, to any page—like those medieval readers who were throwing the *sortes vergilianae*, seeking answers from the poet regarded as a magus, whose wisdom can help with life's questions—and pick up the story and its hero for as long as I wish. The Bishop-Lowell correspondence makes for a kind of dual biography, best read from front to back, but for someone who knows the poets and their work, it is legitimate to open and read anywhere. The poets' letters answer one another, but each entry has a life of its own. "Tolle, lege": the words of Saint Augustine come to mind. "Lift, read": it is the classic formula because the simplest. Begin here. Begin anywhere. Then continue. Stop. Begin again.

Except for trips and vacations by road, train, or air, I have put aside long works of fiction in favor of shorter works or others, like those I mention above, that can be dipped into. The Big Book ("Big

Book, Big Evil," said the smart third-century B.C.E. Greek poet Callimachus) still beckons, but it also intimidates. I resist its siren's call unless I can find optimal conditions in which to hear it. Wallace Stevens once said that a long poem "comes to possess the reader and . . . naturalizes him in its own imagination and liberates him there." True enough, and equally true for long works of prose. Time remains the necessary ally as well as the enemy. You need a lot of it. Virginia Woolf advised would-be readers to avoid entirely Spenser's *Faerie Queene*: "Put it off as long as possible." She continues with a list of mundane activities to pursue instead, "and then, when the whole being is red and brittle as sandstone in the sun, make a dash for *The Faery Queen* and give yourself up to it." As with many long books, the best time and place for such self-sacrifice, abandoning oneself to a book, is when one is laid up in bed with an illness that incapacitates mildly but does not impair one's faculties, something that involves immobility, maybe a few light drugs, and little pain. A broken leg, with a little traction, perhaps.

We seldom have that kind of time. Brevity becomes the soul of wisdom and passion, as well as wit. My preferred tastes now run to shorter things. No longer Joyce and James, except for their stories and novellas, no longer Proust, but Willa Cather, William Maxwell, and Peter Taylor among twentieth-century novelists, or any other master of cool clarity, sharpened perception, and a transparent style, the art that hides art. William Trevor, Alice Munro, and John Cheever come to mind: masters of short fiction whose power takes hold immediately but subtly, drawing one in, and both captures and—in Stevens's phrase—liberates. Or other writers, now well beyond middle age, who can show us the way and reveal what lies ahead. I think of the English octogenarian Jane Gardam. And I try to be fair to those younger writers—Edward St. Aubyn, Caleb Crain, and Jhumpa Lahiri can stand in for many others—whose work gives fresh, unexpected pleasures and lets us in on what the new generations are up to.

At least as important as genre or length are tone and style. For me, a senior reader, the sentence matters, perhaps most of all. Lucidity now trumps opacity and difficulty. I understand, as my younger self did not, that complexity is not synonymous with depth, nor simplicity with superficiality. Style makes its own demands. I badger my students with my definition of good writing: it is what makes you interested in something you are not interested in. Quality of syntax and language indicates quality of mind. The unexpected adjective, or a surprising adjective-noun combination, can jump from the page into a reader's mind.

Edith Wharton, master of nuance and social detail, can take one's breath away with the simplest gesture. Here's one such unobtrusive, easy-to-miss sentence that, on the one hand, has nothing to do with the action of the narrative and, on the other hand, everything to do with the mind of a character. A man has embarked on an illicit love affair that will have terrible consequences as the novel progresses. At the theater in Paris, he is happy to be seen with a beautiful woman on his arm in a public place where no one will recognize them. But "happy" is not how Wharton limns her man: "Darrow, lighting a cigarette while she sucked her straw, knew the primitive complacency of the man at whose companion other men stare" (*The Reef*). "Primitive" is an unanticipated but accurate choice, especially in combination with "complacency." Wharton, the astute observer of manners and morals, has depicted the essential crudeness at the root of a sophisticated masculine psychology. Men, she seems to say to us, they're all the same, wherever and whenever you find them.

Two favorite contemporary writers, one still alive, the other recently gone, both octogenarians, have written their final books. Shirley Hazzard and James Salter can insinuate thoughts and feelings quirkily or with unforeseen turns of phrase, unexpected metaphors, off stylistic gestures. This gift alone can keep a reader going. Through its style even more than its subjects, Salter's memoir *Burn-*

ing the Days opens up to us its author's paradoxical feline heterosexuality, a combination of Hemingway's cool machismo and James's subtleties of perception. Here is Salter on the eternal erotic promise of Rome, following his inventories of the available women and the louche men who pursue them:

> It was a city of matchless decrepitude: muted colors, fountains, trees on the rooftops, beautiful tough boys, trash. A southern city—there were palms on the Piazza di Spagna and the sun incandescent in the afternoon. A venal city, flourishing through the ages—nothing so often betrayed could retain a shred of illusion. In the day it was beautiful. At night it became sinister.

One moves forward through the prose, stopping to admire the adjectives ("matchless" and "muted" linked through alliteration; "beautiful" and "tough" linked through opposition), to realize that the city is like a person, capable of being betrayed, and lacking all illusion. The city becomes its people—beautiful by day, sinister by night. Any page of Salter can sound like this. His last novel, *All That Is*, proves that great masters in their late styles can strip away everything inessential to reveal necessary essences. Late Matisse cutouts come to mind.

There is not a single sentence of Shirley Hazzard's—regardless of her subjects—that has not afforded me pleasure. Whether writing about meeting Graham Greene on Capri or her early days working at the United Nations, she has an arresting way of making you pause and moving you forward. Here is the opening paragraph of *The Great Fire*, her splendid novel about the aftermath of World War II:

> Now they were starting. Finality ran through the train, an exhalation. There were thuds, hoots, whistles, and the shrieks of late arrivals. From a megaphone, announcements were incomprehensible in American and Japanese. Before the train had moved at

all, the platform faces receded into the expression of those who remain.

What is the appeal? First of all, the verbs, none of which is transitive and some of which are passive, or mere verbs of being. This is the kind of writing Strunk and White and other master teachers and editors always caution against. Hazzard is holding us back but also priming us for action. Second, the wonderful combination, almost a paradox, of "starting" and "finality" in the first two sentences. Something is coming to an end, right here at the beginning. Next, instead of "English," the unexpected "American," to remind us of the war just finished and the political-military stakes. (The novel begins in Japan. The year is 1947.) It identifies the conquerors. Last, most surprising but technically correct, the single present-tense verb at the end of the paragraph: "those who remain." The people on the platform—rather, their faces, like "the apparition of these faces in a crowd" memorably caught by Pound in his famous imagist poem—have been transformed into an abstract, allegorical, universal group. No longer the people at this particular station, they have become any group being left behind. Hazzard has started with a specific time and place; she has also opened us up to another world, of almost mythic, universal dimensions.

By instinct and profession, I am a reader and critic of poetry. I am always looking for new poets or rereading the works of the great ones who inspired me when I was young. Everyone's tastes, in literature, music, art, and food, change with age. Some preferences remain, while others drop away. Those perennial favorites of adolescents—Dylan Thomas and E. E. Cummings—don't do much for me anymore, other than remind me of my earlier self. But anyone who wants to introduce junior high school students to the power and intricacies of poetry could not go wrong with their poems. In college, enthralled by the opacities of modernism, I was deaf to the beauty of Whitman. Now, at the other end of my life, I can see and hear why he is—bloviation and repetition aside—the great American genius, as capable of tenderness, sadness, and delicacy as his contemporary Emily Dickinson is capable of tough vigor and hardheaded composure.

A great twentieth-century intellectual once said, "I read poetry because it saves time." That was Marilyn Monroe. Poetry makes its mark and engages its readers in two complementary ways: through condensation and expansive suggestiveness. It packs its power, meanings, and effects into the fewest number of words, but it encourages each reader to respond to, and thereby to interpret, the evidence individually, even idiosyncratically. A phrase, figure of speech, syntactic arrangement, musical gesture, will affect each reader differently. Reading a poem takes less time than reading prose, but with a poem, as with a picture or a song, you have the advantage, even the obligation, of repeating the experience. Eye and ear take in the same data more than once. The work seeps in: you can memorize poems, long as well as short ones, without even trying to. The clever people who devised the Poetry in Motion series for subways and buses knew that a haiku, a sonnet, anything contained in a poster at or above eye level, can both stimulate and sedate the mind of a passenger who is hypnotically looking.

Dr. Johnson said of *Paradise Lost* that no one ever wished it longer. One definition of a classic is a book that everyone wants to have read, not necessarily wants to reread. But I can pick up Milton or Virgil, open at random, begin reading, and stop whenever I wish. The classics renew themselves with repetition. A part can count for almost as much as the whole.

As a reader, I have had good luck. First of all, I still read. This is the activity to which I am most addicted. Not doing it—like not exercising—for even a short time provokes twitchiness and withdrawal. Next, now that I am reading fewer and shorter novels, and reading fiction of any sort less frequently than I do nonfictional prose and poetry, I can happily match my tastes to my capacity.

The brevity of poetry is only part of its appeal. If I sought brevity alone, I would fit right into the twenty-first century, but of course I do not. I have never written, and only rarely read, a tweet. I have never looked at, let alone appeared on, Facebook. I seldom read anyone's blog. I have too many books I need to read, and to read again. I'll leave tweeting to the young. I asked a class of students last year, "How much time do you spend each day on social media?" Two of them said virtually simultaneously, "About forty-five minutes."

"You're lying," I shot back. They admitted I was right. When class ended and they all immediately turned their cell phones on, I asked one young woman how many messages she'd received during the previous eighty minutes. "Twenty-two," she said.

"How many require immediate attention, or attention at all?"

"Only one, not immediate but by the end of the day: from my mother."

I asked a group of high school students last spring how many of them spent time doing "free" reading, reading not assigned for class. They all raised their hands. I was impressed. Queried further, they said that the bulk of such reading was stuff written by their friends: they meant text messages, tweets, and blogs. Whether this ought to be cause for celebration or regret remains to be learned. Better to read something than nothing at all, I suppose, but I have books.

"By their books ye shall know them": I take this motto seriously. On a recent three-and-a-half-hour plane trip, I walked through what the pilot always helpfully refers to as the "aircraft" twice: once, forty minutes after takeoff, and once forty minutes before landing. One hundred and forty-four people filled the main cabin. Fifteen were reading books or something on their e-readers and Kindles. An equal number were reading magazines, and not of the *New York Review* sort. Others were playing video games, looking at movies on their personal computers, watching the in-flight entertainment, or just sleeping. The percentages seemed about right, what I probably would have guessed beforehand.

I was certainly the only person on board who was reading Wordsworth's *Prelude*. Perhaps I am the only person ever to read it on an American Airlines flight. Sitting cramped in my seat, I contemplated Wordsworth's account of his first year at university. From his undergraduate rooms, the young poet, a mediocre student at Cambridge, saw at Trinity College the statue of Newton "with his prism and silent face, / The marble index of a mind for ever / Voyaging through strange seas of thought, alone." Flying through the air, I was, like all readers, also moving through my own seas of thought, alone among strangers, and grateful for my solitude.

ART ☙

One can read a book anywhere, in virtually any conditions, in a crowd or alone in a quiet room. Even in a crowd—unless reading aloud to an audience, sharing an experience with others—every reader is a solitary. This is not the case, for the most part, with the other arts. One can listen to music alone, at home, with eyes shut and ears open. Seldom is one alone with a picture. To look at paintings, unless one is a wealthy collector, means sharing space with other people in public spaces. The pleasures of museums, as everyone knows, are balanced by the inevitable irritations we endure when we walk through the door. One virtue any senior citizen ought to possess is patience, and that patience will be sorely tested in almost any picture gallery.

Everyone knows the feeling: discomfort, annoyance, rage, an entire range of emotions provoked by other people when one might wish to have total solitude, or at least relative peace and quiet. Welcome to the modern museum experience.

What do we want when confronting great art? Books are easy, ready companions, and it's always possible to block out other distractions by resorting to noise-reducing devices that insulate us with auditory privacy. With film, live music, and especially theater, the audience and its collective responses contribute to the greater pleasure of attending, even though there are plenty of times when one wants to smack the people sitting behind, talking as though they were in their living room; or glare angrily at the woman with dangling jewelry and poisonous perfume in the next seat; or strangle the coughing man on the other side who is noisily unwrapping his lozenges. Rock concerts depend on mass participation; classical ones, formerly the closest thing to silent worship you could find outside a church, are starting to resemble them as they become more like pop events. Not wanting to intimidate younger audiences, classical music producers now aim for more nonthreatening, interactive experiences. The concert event is more like a warm bath than a challenge. In some venues, the players now chat with the audience, and the audience is encouraged to applaud when it wants, not just at the end of a piece or even at the end of a movement. This allows people to express themselves, to show their appreciation.

The fact that one person's applause or cheer might interfere with his neighbor's listening seems of little importance. In most cities, like Dallas, where I live, everything warrants a standing ovation with whoops and barks and hollers. Someone will leap to his feet and make enthusiastic noise. Why? Presumably to show appreciation; or is it to feel good about his expenditure of big money for a ticket and to let his neighbors see that he is among the cognoscenti? If someone in front of you stands up, then you are required to stand as well if you want to see the stage. In Europe, polite applause is still standard practice. I doubt this will last much longer. The greatest testimony to the power of a musical performance is silence. At the opera, why can people not wait at least for the last note to resonate, for the curtain to descend, before breaking into their self-congratulatory applause?

We can no longer depend on the old-fashioned traditions of the concert hall for moments of transcendent silence. This leaves the visual arts. The aim, at least my highest aim, is a private, solitary contemplation of a single work, in silence and through time. Studies have confirmed my unscientific sense that the average looker spends no more than fifteen seconds in front of any painting. People wander through museums, aimlessly, listlessly: watch them looking and you can see for yourself. What I call the "act of looking"—it is, after all, an action—means not a passive glance by a fast-moving tourist equipped with an audio guide and a camera but an extended act of reciprocal absorption. This is what I always hope for. Sometimes my hopes are dashed by my own inadequacies or temperament—the mind wanders, the tedious details of life interrupt my attention—but more often than not it is the sheer unpleasantness of the museum experience that inhibits, indeed prohibits, active looking. Art is of the body, and if you are too hot or cold, if you have a headache or hangover, you're certainly not going to think or feel at your highest level. And when other people get in the way, as they always do, so much the worse.

The goal of the real aesthete is not necessarily ownership but intimacy, to which ownership is often the surest course. I wonder, however, what percentage of collectors in today's price-driven market actually sit in quiet before their Picasso, Rothko, or Jeff Koons. They may be calculating its resale value next year. But I also think of the Duke of Ferrara in Robert Browning's "My Last Duchess," who pulls aside the curtain on the portrait of his dead wife for his visitor, thereby ensuring control over the young woman who was too easily pleased, too kind to everyone else, too non-discriminating, and too unappreciative of his family's name and status when she was alive. Now he owns her two-dimensional substitute, which he need not share if he does not choose to. A student who tacks onto a dormitory wall the most clichéd of Modigliani or Klimt posters knows the pleasures of private looking. And even the least successful reproduction retains something of what Walter Benjamin called the "aura" of an original artwork. For the purpose of contemplation, authenticity and originality do not count for much. In the quiet of that cell-block dormitory room, a ten-dollar print can inspire intimacies with art unavailable in most museum galleries. You may not be able to gauge the delicacies of the original work—brushstrokes, impasto, color, other nuances—but an ersatz reproduction can generate an authentic response even in a student who lacks the skills or opportunities of a connoisseur. You do not need to see close-up the evidence of the artist's hand to have something like a spiritual experience. You get to think about your picture. It becomes a part of you. In your effort to decorate, to beautify your room, to make it your own, you have defined yourself by a single choice. We can call this an act of self-determination. We can call it style.

In the museum, noise is always the biggest deterrent to such intimacies. But the overheard conversations of people who have forgotten to use what our mothers helpfully referred to as "indoor voices" sometimes attest amusingly to the democracy of wandering and of sharing space and time with fellow citizens. Many years ago, I went to a show of Chinese bronzes from the People's Republic at the Metropolitan Museum. Flanking the grand entrance to the galleries was a pair of Ming dynasty vases, perched on ornate rosewood stands and embossed with dragons and delicately rich floral patterns. They stood four and a half feet high. Before me, two earnest Manhattan ladies of a recognizable sort—well coiffed, wearing good jewelry—strolled in. They eyeballed the urns.

"Gorgeous," said the first.

"But where would I put them?" asked the second. This was the entirety of their exchange.

This pair was not Joseph Duveen and J. P. Morgan, but they were the bourgeois, domesticated descendants of buyers and collectors from the Gilded Age. For these ladies and their like, all art aspires to the condition of the living room. Ownership, or the thought, the possibility, of ownership, occupies their engagement with the things they see. Art is part of decor. There is nothing wrong, or even embarrassing, with thinking this way. When my mother decided that it was time to buy an oil picture for our modest living room, she consulted a more sophisticated friend—another suburban yenta but one with airs—who worked part-time in the art business. Estelle claimed familiarity with real painters; she had brushed up against local greatness. She took my mother to a Philadelphia gallery where they surveyed the merchandise. My mother opted for a perfectly ordinary seascape—waves and clouds, water and air, a sunset peering through, and some seagulls to suggest movement—and told Estelle how much she liked the picture. "And the colors will match my sofa," she said, triumphantly making her point. Shades of blue and green and white: the picture was perfect for a brick colonial home of a half century ago.

"Oh, no," said Estelle, "you should never buy a painting because it will complement the decor." I realized only years later that my mother was as right in her opinion as her more hoity-toity consultant was in hers. Why not think of the living room as a *Gesamtkunstwerk*, an entire, organically conceived work of art? If people as diverse as Goethe, Kandinsky, and Josef Albers can consider and write seriously about theories of color, why should an untaught middle-class lady not be allowed to respond to art through this most basic of criteria, this most central of pleasures? We respond to colors in ways that are elementary and therefore deep. This large, unimpressive oil followed my parents from our house to successive apartments in their retirement. It gave them happiness. What else should a picture do? I think it may still live, along with some still lifes by a couple of our Sunday-painting great-aunts, in my brother's basement, a buried legacy from parents to children who will neither dispose of it nor enjoy it.

I have gone to museums with a pair of married friends, she a sociologist, he a literary man. They insist on playing this little game: You walk into a room at the museum, and you ask yourself which picture you want to bring home with you. Then you debate the issue with one another. Why this one, and not that one? Please discuss. A whole world of tastes and ideas opens up.

For sheer scholarly sobriety, a different kind of looker is a serious art writer I have met, who also, owing to family wealth, owns important twentieth-century paintings. She can afford to think of both the works themselves and the spaces they will occupy in her Manhattan apartment overlooking the East River. She was preparing a book on contemporary museum architecture and design, a study of new American art buildings and collections. A mutual friend asked whether she was going to consider the issue of traffic patterns, the flow and movement of visitors, in museum spaces, and she looked at him quizzically, as if hearing of a bizarre, or at least novel, issue. "Traffic patterns?" she asked.

And then he realized: she had seldom if ever gone to museums when other people, or at least too many other people, shared her space. The doors open for her at special, private hours; her guides are not the helpful, solicitous docents, some better trained than others, who instruct schoolchildren and members of hoi polloi, but the chief curators of the collections. Neither traffic nor human noise will stay the slow completion of her appointed rounds, nor otherwise interrupt her private experience of the art.

Everyone who looks at art seriously can count the times he or she has had the accidental good fortune of privacy. In an encyclopedic museum—the Metropolitan, the Louvre, the Prado, the National Galleries in London and Washington—all you usually need is a stroll out of the clogged thoroughfares, the space in front of, say, the *Mona Lisa*, herself triply protected by museum guards, her position behind a bulletproof frame, and the rail that cordons her off from the hundreds of cell-phone-photograph-snapping tourists. These eager aficionados are the equivalent of the madly applauding concertgoers leaping to their feet at the end of a performance. They are congratulating themselves. These days, instead of photographing the paintings, they are making selfies, pictures of themselves with masterpieces behind them. They have turned their backs on the very art other people wish to confront head-on. Why are they doing this? Certainly not to remind themselves of what the *Mona Lisa* looks like. Postcards used to be aides-mémoire. The selfie now gets posted to one's Facebook friends. "Here I am," it says, "with her!" Who is the main subject here? The touring viewer herself has not seen Leonardo's picture at all. She has held her camera at arm's length, and the painting is, consequently, still farther away. And her intended audience: Does anyone really care about someone else's vacation?

My advice to serious museumgoers is to come in thirty or forty minutes before closing time, when the crowds are thinning. You will always have more privacy. Even better: Leave the great long gallery. Take a path less traveled. I have walked into the Chardin galleries at the Louvre a handful of times and spent an hour with little or no interruption meditating on this master of the everyday, beloved of Proust and of everyone else with an eye for still life, *nature morte*, the arrangements of ordinary items, what Wallace Stevens might have called planets on a table. Every encyclopedic museum boasts treasures hidden away, pieces of art in styles and forms you never even heard of. Take a good long look at them. Serendipity, when your eyes are open, can ravish you. All pictures are little worlds, cunningly made. One measure of artistic greatness is the capacity of a work of art to inspire long, thoughtful, responsive meditation in a viewer. This is also the measure of the viewers themselves.

And then there have been the delicious, unpredictable occasions when I have become like the lady art historian with connections and had the good fortune of momentary solitude, sometimes with a single work, or a small room, or an entire museum. Twice in the past five years, I have visited Frank Furness's neo-Gothic Victorian masterpiece, the Pennsylvania Academy of the Fine Arts, in Philadelphia, my hometown. Both times, I was practically the only person in any of the galleries. "How sad!" said a Philadelphia friend.

"Not for me," I quickly replied. Sad for revenues, public relations, and everything else the Academy's front office counts on, but what could be better than being alone in picture-laden rooms with no noise and no other bodies to compete with one's silent looking at Winslow Homer, Thomas Eakins, and Richard Diebenkorn?

Once I persuaded a kindly or perhaps just lackadaisical guard at the Brera Museum in Milan to let me pull up a heavy chair from the sidelines so I could sit and look undisturbed at Piero della Francesca's Montefeltro Altarpiece, a Madonna and Child with surrounding saints. He even granted me the probably illegal privilege of momentarily walking behind a metal guardrail to get a real close-up look. Italian guards seem to epitomize and perpetuate the clichés about the national character. Their generosity belongs to a more haphazard sense of order: random, chaotic, antiauthoritarian, and spur-of-the-moment. We like to think of this as charmingly Mediterranean. Sometimes it works to a tourist's advantage.

Membership, as the old credit card advertisement used to brag, also has its privileges. The Dallas Museum of Art sends out occasional e-mail notices to members of a certain status ("partners") announcing "Quiet Viewing Hours Just for You." My latest letter gave me a two-hour time frame, 5:30 to 7:30 one Tuesday evening several weeks in the future. Museums are enforcing an unsubtle distinction between plebeians who must endure less than ideal conditions and first-class customers who deserve first-class viewing rights. Quiet is not a right but something to purchase. A cynic might simply say, "You get what you pay for." At the Museum of Modern

Art, normally as quiet a spot as Bloomingdale's, museum members may come at 9:30 before the crowds. One recent Saturday morning, a gorgeous September fall day in Manhattan, I was the first person to enter the museum. I made my race to the fifth floor and spent an entire hour in the Matisse room. There I was, alone with ten great paintings, including *The Red Studio* and *The Piano Lesson*. This time my great revelation came to me during the full twenty minutes I spent in front of the vast picture *The Moroccans* (1915–16) as I focused my attention exclusively on the eye-catching palette on the picture's right side: a field of lavender turning to mauve, abutting another mass of terra-cotta and salmon, with blue and yellow accents pulling the eye to other parts of the picture.

My eyes were awash with color.

And on my only visit to Berlin, a couple of years ago, I showed up at the Kunstgewerbemuseum, a treasure trove of the decorative arts, when it opened in the morning, and for two hours I had the splendid, slightly surreal experience of being one of only two people in this miraculous hall of textiles, panels, ceramics, industrial design, objects religious and secular, everything ranging from the medieval period through art deco. Total, unexpected silence complemented the experience of looking at the hundreds of striking, mysterious things that had long since outlived their usefulness. I felt that I was in a toy shop, a tomb, or perhaps in tchotchke heaven. The Germans have a word for such displays: *Wunderkammern*, rooms filled with wonderful items. Originally these were rooms for natural curiosities, geological and biological finds, but increasingly they took on a more domestic character.

What added to my pleasure was the fact that all the wall labels were in only one language. I had to rely on the remnants of my vestigial schoolboy German to get at the essence of the descriptions. In the age of multilingual audio guides, of the understandable efforts of arts organizations to make experiences and objects more accessible to visitors, viewers, and listeners, there was something wondrous indeed about seeing case after case filled with things like a *Doppelturmofen,* a *Türklopfer,* a *Schälchen mit Blütendekor,* an *Elefanten-Giessgefäss,* and many *Deckelpokale,* not to mention things whose uses as well as histories remained tantalizingly vague.

That my job was not easy made it all the more exciting. Far from diminishing the fun, too little information added to the curious bewilderment I was experiencing. I had to work harder to see and to understand. I'm not sure how much I understood or retained through my acts of looking, but the process made me a little tipsy. Because I could not learn the history, the purpose, or the relevance of any single object, I had to become a total aesthete: I had to rely on my eyes alone to get a grasp on what a thing was, not what it meant, and to focus on what it looked like, rather than how it functioned. These objects, I thought, had been removed from their raisons d'être; now they just sat there, waiting to be admired. Did they, I wondered, talk it over among themselves at night, regretting that they could no longer serve as objects of use to those families who had commissioned, or bought, and cared for them, who polished and sharpened them? I thought of Colette's *L'enfant et les sortilèges* and the Disney cartoon *Toy Story,* in which the toys do exactly that. The Berlin museum had promoted these things to the higher status of "art" from the lowlier one of "craft." At least that is how one experienced them in the absence of additional knowledge. Formerly, they served a purpose. Now they sat empty of meaning, and if they were a flagon, a cabinet, or a tea service, they were empty, as well, of their intended contents. These containers had been themselves contained within the museum. They were things no longer. They were objects in cabinets, behind glass, or under spotlights begging us to think about and appreciate them.

Ignorance opens us up to such unplanned, weird imaginings. When both spoken and written language—words heard, overheard, or read—prove inaccessible, the other senses must take over. And to have such an experience occur virtually apart from all other people meant that the entire museum, a cabinet of wonders writ large, belonged to me alone. Solitude and silence heighten almost all artistic experiences. For a brief time, you can become the monarch of all you survey.

Many museumgoers can tell similar stories, however infrequent. Standing or sitting still, looking long and hard, is a rare enough phenomenon, becoming rarer still in an age of edutainment when museums prefer, or feel compelled, to shuttle through their doors the busloads of schoolchildren and tourists who require a flicker of enlightenment before proceeding to their day's next event or episode. Whatever art does these days, it seldom does it to isolated individuals, in quiet. Just as the hushed tones of libraries have long since vanished, so also indoor voices—more available in Europe than in the States—are being drowned out.

How about an art exhibit titled, simply, *Silence*? An odd occurrence, certainly, but one that I visited. Silence is now as precious and rare as slowness or solitude, clean air, and a star-filled night sky (see "Quiet," starting on page 167). As someone who never goes anywhere without earplugs, and who would rather stay hungry than be forced into a noisy restaurant, I was keen to visit *Silence* at Houston's Menil Collection in 2013. In a variety of tones, voices, and media, it reminded me of what we often want but can never have.

You could not experience silence there. That would be impossible, even in the cool, chaste chambers of Renzo Piano's exquisite building. This exhibit was really a riff on the late John Cage's remark "There's no such thing as silence." The show had fifty-two pieces. Some were conventional paintings by de Chirico, Magritte, Rauschenberg, and Rothko, all favorites of John and Dominique de Menil, who had amassed a quirky collection before their museum opened in 1987.

Hanging on the walls were other two-dimensional works, like Yves Klein's vibrant, glistening, gold leaf *Untitled (Monogold)*. Sculpture, small objects, neon tubing, other three-dimensional art, complemented the pictures. The show featured audio and video installations and a living performance piece by Tino Sehgal, in which a dancer rolled slowly along the floor of an interior room for two and a half hours, followed by another dancer who did the same thing. It certainly was silent, gripping in a boring kind of way.

A typical museum show often moves chronologically; in a thematic show, organizers make other arrangements. *Silence* might have seemed random, but it had a partially recognizable plan. After a vestibule containing a selection of representative works, you entered four inner rooms. The first, the most conventional and tightly arranged, was in many ways the most moving. Four Andy Warhol pieces—silk-screened ink and acrylic on linen from the mid-1960s—represented the ultimate silence, death, in this case death by electrocution. Warhol's depictions of the electric chair at Sing Sing are beautiful, almost abstract in their wash of color, a kind of phantom homage to Jackson Pollock. The smallest one, *Little Electric Chair,* is so black that you might have mistaken it for a cousin to Ad Reinhardt's all-black *Abstract Painting* in another room, until you came close and saw the chiseled outline of the electric chair staring right back at you.

Interspersed among the Warhols were seven silk screens by Christian Marclay (2006), each focusing on the single word "Silence" above the electric chair in the death chamber. Silence surrounded the viewer, at least visually, on all sides.

The other rooms contained miscellaneous pieces. Some "talked" to one another; others seemed more randomly placed. Dominique de Menil, a woman of austere and religious character, famously said that "only silence and love do justice to a great work of art," but this show hardly permitted silence. Interrupting a private contemplation of the art were not only the voices and footsteps of other viewers but also the sounds from the audio installations, including, most boomingly, Kurt Mueller's *Cenotaph* (2011), an old jukebox into which you put a quarter and then got to hear one of ninety-nine moments of silence, all of which were preceded by very noisy introductions. No silence comes without sound.

In many ways, the most compelling pieces were two video installations, each within its own darkened chamber. Jacob Kirkegaard's 2006 *AION* (Greek for eternity or infinity) was shot on location in ruined spaces at Chernobyl, site of a terrifying 1986 nuclear reactor explosion. Shapes and colors move, come in and out of focus; an interior landscape is bathed in light, then dark shadows, then overwhelmed with whiteness. Static architecture changes as though it were tai chi, Keats's "slow time" reimagined.

If you moved counterclockwise through the show, the last thing you saw was the most resonant, a return to John Cage, silence's major spokesman. On August 29, 1952, David Tudor sat down at a piano and performed for the first time Cage's now iconic (or fraudulent, depending on one's point of view) *4'33"*: a work in three movements and total silence other than the extraneous sounds within the hall. Cage himself said it could be "played" by any soloist or group of players.

Manon de Boer's *Two Times "4'33""* stars Jean-Luc Fafchamps. We see him at his piano—stern, unblinking, virtually motionless—and we hear him set and release the chess timer that marks the three movements. A plate glass window behind him gives onto wintry snow and ice. He sits, he waits, he finishes, and then he stands up. An unseen audience applauds.

The film resumes. This time, we hear the timer's clicks, but now we watch not the pianist but his rapt audience of earnest, attentive young people. And we see another view to the outside: a northern European city (it's Brussels, December 2, 2007), part industrial, part architectural, part natural.

To reach de Boer's installation in Houston, you had to walk through two heavy doors with sound-deadening panels and two sets of heavy black draperies. There, you sat on a bench, with a single light above you. The chamber was dark. You were bathed in silence, except for the sounds of the jukebox outside, which intruded whenever someone put a quarter in the old nickelodeon.

Cage would have been pleased. There is no silence in a museum, but somehow the very thought of it can take you out of yourself. And for some reason, the very title and substance of the show encouraged or inspired museumgoers to move with gentler treads and to speak, if at all, more softly than usual.

This was the kind of miracle that happens every so often. The crowds vanish. Perhaps no one is around to begin with, as was the case for me in Philadelphia. Or perhaps something impressive so transports the viewer that he can forget the crowds, noisy or inconvenient though they may be. If you want to look carefully at the ceiling of the Sistine Chapel, rather than be whisked through on a peremptory visit, you must steel yourself and try to press from your mind everything that is not Michelangelo: the noise, the people, the jostling. Wait for a seat on the periphery, and then grab it. Crane your neck. Look your fill. Wait for another seat on another side of the room. Move around. At New York's Frick Collection in January 2014, I waited for a spot to open, and I planted myself in front of Vermeer's *Girl with a Pearl Earring*, on loan from the Mauritshuis in The Hague, until I had satisfied myself. I steadied myself and ignored my raucous, elbowing neighbors. I knew that my selfish stationary posture annoyed some of my fellow viewers, who wanted to get a better position in front of the painting. I did not give way. I made everyone else move around me or wait his turn to take my place. Viewing can be difficult; it can be unpleasant. You must be willing to suffer to take the measure of the work at hand. And you must be selfish and cause others to suffer for your enjoyment.

The thrill of slow looking—I use the term as a relative to slow food and slow, close reading—has also occurred when I come to an art exhibition that changes my mind about an artist I never knew well: Willem de Kooning, Arshile Gorky, and Wassily Kandinsky most recently. Or that introduces me to an artist of whom I have previously known nothing at all: Howard Hodgkin, years ago, first in Fort Worth and then at the Metropolitan Museum; Antonio López García at Boston's Museum of Fine Arts; L. S. Lowry at Tate Britain several summers ago. A world opens itself up and invites you in. The surroundings melt, and it's just you and the pictures. These things happen. Keats described the experience as feeling that a new planet has swum into your ken. He was thinking of literature—in his case George Chapman's translation of Homer— but the analogy obtains.

And at least once, for me, the audience was part of the experience and not a deterrent to it. The event was musical, so although it re-sembled what happens in a symphony hall, an opera house, or even a rock concert, its own uniqueness overwhelmed the attendees, who turned out to be not so much an audience as participants in a shared experience. I watched them, and as we all listened to the same sounds, T. S. Eliot's lines from "The Dry Salvages" never seemed more applicable: "music heard so deeply / That it is not heard at all, but you are the music / While the music lasts."

In December 2013, I went to the Cloisters, the Metropolitan Museum's serene medieval outpost at the top of Manhattan. I wanted to see and hear the sound installation by the Canadian artist Janet Cardiff. That first experience encouraged me to repeat it a week later. On two visits, ninety minutes each, I stood in a Spanish chapel listening to music. What was it? In 2001, Cardiff made a recording at Salisbury Cathedral of Thomas Tallis's mid-sixteenth-century polyphonic motet *Spem in alium* for forty voices. She lined the walls with curtains and blankets to control the sound and to deaden the space. Nineteen additional children augmented the forty called-for singers. All fifty-nine musicians wore lavaliere microphones attached to cables that ran to a truck outside. Then, combining some of the children's parts, she reduced the audio tracks to forty. The eleven-minute piece, officially owned by the National

Gallery of Canada in Ottawa, has been staged in many venues around the world, the Cloisters being the most recent and also the best and most appropriate of them. In all sites, forty audio speakers—one for each voice—are positioned in a room. At the Cloisters' Fuentidueña Chapel, a limestone Spanish apse from the twelfth century, the work was "performed" continuously throughout the day over a three-month period. This was the first time the Cloisters had hosted any contemporary art, although the essence of the Tallis polyphonic piece is hardly modern. The whole experience combined the old and the new. It was actually neither old nor new. Instead, it offered a taste of eternity.

The drill was easy. You stood somewhere, anywhere, in the chapel. The loudspeakers, mounted on stands and divided into eight groups of five (one for each of the vocal types: bass, baritone, tenor, alto, soprano), made an oval in the apse. The music began. Eleven minutes later, it ended. Between "performances," you listened, if you so chose, to three minutes of chatter among and between the choristers. Then the tape resumed. The idea for this continuous loop is as simple as can be. You start by listening to ordinary secular life, which then ends and miraculously gives way once the first sonorous bass voice sings "Spem," and life of a different order begins. The gap between the chatter and the music might have provided the biggest jolt of all. Over the course of my twelve fourteen-minute cycles, I heard a full range of uninteresting exchanges, gossip, pleasantries (what Yeats called "polite meaningless words" in his poem "Easter, 1916") among the singers: "That line there got me messed up"; "In the end, where we turn the page from 19 to 20, we always get that wrong"; "Oh, you're back?"; "We'll do our very best and then give you a breather . . . and there's water"; "His last moments were spent recording *Spem in alium*"; "Hmmm"; plus noises of throats clearing, pages turning, a man humming, a tuning fork, a yawn, and pure vocalise. I felt I had entered into a meandering

John Ashbery poem, with many frequencies of speech flowing right along. We were not so much hearing as overhearing this prelude to the concert.

A helpful guard told me to position myself at the music stand of the first bass singer, toward the room's entrance. At the end of the three-minute chitchat, that singer's voice ever so gently intoned "Let's rock," which was—as I learned once I had moved around the circle many times—simultaneous with other singers saying things like "Okay, let's give it a whirl" and "Let's give it our best shot. We've worked very hard." The sudden transition, virtually unprepared for, from the ordinary or the secular to the transcendent or the divine took place in an unheralded moment. The only equivalent I can think of is Louis Malle's *Vanya on 42nd Street*, a film of a Chekhov production that never actually saw the light of day. The movie begins with stage actors emerging from the subway and the street and walking into the theater for rehearsal. They chat on the largely vacant stage, and then, without so much as a curtain rise or a "Let's start now," they transport themselves, and us, to the world of nineteenth-century Russia. The recent Globe performances of *Twelfth Night* on Broadway did the same, in this case taking us to Shakespeare's fictive Illyria and his actual London, but stage music alerted the audience to the main event.

At the Cardiff installation, Tallis's music existed in space as well as time. You stood at one end of the apse or the other, or you stood in the middle of the floor. The term "surround sound" never seemed more appropriate. Better still, you moved from speaker to speaker to experience the individual voices one at a time. Best of all, you stood between speakers, between baritone and tenor or between alto and soprano. Or you performed some combination of all of the above. The possibilities were almost infinite. You would not hear the same rendition twice if you wanted a different one. Not everyone sings at once. And they are all singing to us, as well as to one another. Moments of vocal silence punctuate the experience. The music could hit you frontally, laterally, or from behind, depending on your location.

Listening, you became undistractedly aware of the other people in the room with you. At a concert venue—pop or classical—you usually sit or stand facing the stage, the pit, and the performers. Even if you are waving your arms, singing and dancing along with the music, taking photographs on your iPhone, you focus on the stage. At the Cloisters, in the 360-degree installation in which everyone is moving around slowly, you became as visually alert to your fellow human beings as you were musically alert to Thomas Tallis. I kept thinking of the French verb for attending a performance: not *attendre*, but *assister à*. Somehow the attendees assisted in bringing the music to life; we were all handmaidens to the performers inside the boxlike speakers.

The visible cast of characters, my fellow listeners, was both various and generic. Diversity was not much in evidence. More women than men had come to the Cloisters, either because it was a weekday or because that's what women do. Sensible shoes, plus fifty or more shades of black and gray, predominated. Both men and women wore parkas, jeans, and tweeds: vibrant scarves from Burberry and Liberty accented sober colors. Almost everyone was white and middle-aged or beyond, except for one young, hand-holding lesbian couple and a total of four small groups of teenagers. One trio peered in at the entrance and then made a hasty getaway. Another quartet came in, whispered to one another, snapped photographs on their cell phones, and skedaddled. They could not adjust to the old music or the fact of slowness—the patient, plodding movements of the adults—and even the technology of the installation did not hold their attention.

The adults performed a far different ritual, all variations on the idea of slow attentiveness. They seemed to take their cue from a stone statue of Saint Joseph twenty feet above us on the wall. He sits with his right hand cupping his cocked ear, as if waiting for sounds, any sound, to waft upward. Down below, the living audience began their advance into receptivity. Most visitors stayed for one circuit of the piece and then took their leave. Some stayed for two. Two women who had entered the museum with me stayed for three cycles. Almost everyone assumed a look and a posture of concentration. Some came in search of tranquillity; others were clearly delighted to have encountered it. Everyone began with a short pause at the entrance, unconsciously acknowledging the passage from one realm to another, and then moved in and through the apse.

Eventually, some sat with bowed heads and closed eyes, either slightly bent over or steadily upright; others gazed into space with eyes wide open but obviously not focusing on the visible surround. I took a photograph of two men on a bench, both balding and gray, but also a pair of yin and yang. One, with his hands on his knees, looked worried. The other, his hands folded in his lap, his eyes open, emitted a sense of grateful contentment. Was this the peace that passeth understanding or an effort to achieve it? The listeners seemed to be contemplating either the ecstasies of the world or its sorrows. Gentle glances and modest smiles predominated. There was little talk; you could see people occasionally speaking to one another, but of course neither human speech nor muffled footsteps could be heard over the music from the speakers.

My second trip was on an even bleaker, cloudy December morning. The apse was lit; the crucifix was glowing. Illumination poured from the high windows; the faded wall frescoes supplemented the color of the human costumes. The real illumination came in the form of sound, not light. Reverberations from the speakers bounced around the room itself. Because Cardiff did not mass all the parts of one voice in one place, the timbres are dispersed, creating a more harmonious, organic experience. The voices came both as individuals and in groups: a reedy tenor, a plummy alto, a sonorous bass, the children.

I became aware, more than on my first visit, of the opposing forces of inundation and uplift, of being surrounded and pierced, of being absorbed while also absorbing. We heard individual voices, plus antiphony—call and response across the space—and, taken as a whole, in the center of the room, the full force of Tallis's polyphony. Just as the music is a composite of soloists, so also the audience is a community of strangers. I was alone in the crowd, but I was also a part of it.

My two visits put me in mind of the American poet Amy Clampitt, whose extraordinary letters I edited a decade ago. She describes a transcendent moment at the Cloisters in a letter to her youngest brother, Philip, dated March 17, 1956:

> After a while, when the music changed to something else, I was mildly aware that while this was going on I had—perhaps for no more than an instant, but there is no measuring this kind of experience—entirely forgotten my own existence. It is the sort of thing that has happened to me a few times in my life, but always before in moments of great excitement and with a kind of incredulity surrounding it like an iron ring. This time there was no iron ring, no excitement, no surprise even, but a serenity so complete that I hardly thought about it just then, I simply took it for granted. Possibly this is what is supposed to take place at baptism—but if baptism it was, it wasn't of water, but of light. By this time it was late afternoon, and with the reflection from the river so bright that you could barely look at it directly, the whole hilltop, the whole world was fairly brimming with radiance. I walked around for a while, looked at the people, and walked to the subway, rather tired, and yet rested too, and pleased with everything.

This version of grace, an epiphany that came to Clampitt in the form of light as Easter weekend was approaching, led mysteriously some days later to her beginning to write poems for the first time since adolescence. Forgetting her existence, getting out of her very self, was a vocational and spiritual transformation of the highest order.

For the final go-round on my second visit to the installation, I stood still in the center of the apse, eyes closed, in *tadasana*, yoga's "mountain" pose. This is not easy to do for eleven minutes. The body sways, then it doesn't. First you begin to lose and then regain your balance. The secret, I discovered, is to keep weight in your heels. Paradoxically, the effort of not moving makes you break a sweat. My experience, analogous to Clampitt's but not as intense, also left me both tired and rested. Until the end of the motet, the whole ensemble has sung together only twice. The noble last movement begins with the word "Respice," sung by all the voices, and the entire chapel resounds with the fullness of the music. The conclusion is a long exhaled chord. Human harmony symbolizes cosmic harmony. The music of the spheres has come down to earth and lifted us up.

As I left the museum after my second visit, I felt two inches taller. And I said to myself, "You'll never experience anything like this again."

I hope I may be wrong.

NOSTALGIA ✍

Nostalgia is the balm of fear.
—DAVID McGLYNN

Nostalgia isn't what it used to be.
—PETER DE VRIES

As he lay dying of cancer in Boston, John Updike composed a sonnet series that ranks with his best writing in verse, and even prose. Clear-sighted, sober, but witty (unlike many deathbed works), the poems acknowledge feelings of wonder and appreciation. The poet looks at his surroundings in the hospital—the equipment, the noise, the doctors and nurses—and he also takes a backward glance at his early years as a schoolboy in Pennsylvania. Here are the second and third sonnets in the sequence titled "Peggy Lutz, Fred Muth 12/13/08":

> Dear friends of childhood, classmates, thank you,
> scant hundred of you, for providing a
> sufficiency of human types: beauty,
> bully, hanger-on, natural,
> twin, and fatso—all a writer needs,
> all there in Shillington, its trolley cars

and little factories, cornfields and trees,
leaf fires, snowflakes, pumpkins, valentines.

To think of you brings tears less caustic
than those the thought of death brings. Perhaps
we meet our heaven at the start and not
the end of life. Even then were tears
and fear and struggle, but the town itself
draped in plain glory the passing days.

∽

The town forgave me for existing; it
included me in Christmas carols, songfests
(though I sang poorly) at the Shillington,
the local movie house. My father stood,
in back, too restless to sit, but everybody
knew his name, and mine. In turn I knew
my Granddad in the overalled town crew.
I've written these before, these modest facts,

but their meaning has no bottom in my mind.
The fragments in their jiggled scope collide
to form more sacred windows. I had to move
to beautiful New England—its triple
deckers, whited churches, unplowed streets—
to learn how drear and deadly life can be.

Shillington gave Updike all he needed as an artist. Like James
Joyce, who fled Dublin but never truly escaped from it, Updike had
to get away to realize that he had met his heaven, ordinary and
imperfect but sufficient to his needs, at the start of his life. His
hometown nurtured the artist as a young man. For such sustenance, Updike was always grateful.

These sonnets are a product of what I can only call intelligent, rational nostalgia. (Nostalgia can be rational?) And they provoke a set of questions both literary and personal. As life lengthens and the future shortens, it makes sense for us to take backward glances. Even younger people with long lives to look forward to are susceptible to the temptation and charm of nostalgia. As I was giving a talk at a university last year, I realized—way too late to change my topic—that an audience filled with undergraduates was precisely the group least likely to appreciate an older person's obsession with the distant past. And yet I had a moderate success. I made them laugh. Better still, afterward, a pleasant nineteen-year-old sophomore said he found the talk thought provoking. "What are you nostalgic for?" I asked.

"When I was a high school sophomore, my track times were so much faster than they are now," he said wistfully.

More recently, I chuckled when I heard the announcer for a college radio station say to his audience, "I'm now going to play a bunch of late '90s indie rock that'll make you nostalgic if you're, like, between twenty-five and thirty years old." His tone combined the appropriate doses of earnestness, world-weariness, and old-fashioned amazement.

Why do some people look to the past? Why do others refuse to? What are the pleasures of "nostalgia"? The word itself has its etymology in the Greek *nostos* (homecoming)+*algia* (pain), but the condition is more multifaceted, combined of equal parts of homesickness, self-indulgence, sentimentality, and an alertness to the genuine, confected, or merely imagined pleasures of former times and ages and different places. In Updike, and many others of us, the pleasure, not the pain, of remembering predominates.

The word, if not the condition, is modern, coined in 1668 by Johannes Hofer as a translation of the German *Heimweh* (homesickness) to describe the depression he witnessed among Swiss mercenaries longing to get home following service abroad. That its

coinage coincides with the beginnings of the ages of Enlightenment, and then of romanticism, suggests that words both come out
of their historical circumstances and affect subsequent conditions.
They respond to cultural stimuli and then create new feelings, or
new articulations of older ones. In *The Future of Nostalgia*, Svetlana
Boym distinguishes between two nostalgias, a "restorative" version,
a longing for return to the favored place, and a "reflective" one, which
is all about irreparable loss. But today, especially in post–World
War II America, the original pain of nostalgia has often been replaced by the diluted pipe-dream pleasures of casual, lolling trips
down memory lane.

I used to think I was the kind of person who relished, if not
reveled in, nostalgia. I didn't necessarily long for the good old days,
but I enjoyed thinking about them. Looking back made me smile,
even chuckle. People who become historians must have a similar
temperament. Now I am not so sure about which direction I want
to look in. And I have begun to think about nostalgia itself, what it
means, what it promises, and what it denies.

The first epigraph to this chapter gives one explanation of nostalgia through a grammatical sleight of hand. Everything depends
on whether we construe "balm of fear" as what a linguist would call
a subjective or an objective genitive. Either nostalgia is the medica-
tion that dissolves anxieties, the salve that rubs clean our wounds,
or it is what fear itself has doled out to trick us into a momentary
release from fear, a condition all the more toxic once it triumphs
and overwhelms us. Either nostalgia placates, or it deceives. My
second epigraph, from Peter De Vries with his tongue only partly
in cheek, reminds us that styles of remembering and forgetting
always change and that the good old days were never what we
thought, that every presumed golden age yearns for the one before
it. Think of Woody Allen's *Midnight in Paris*, with befuddled, myo-
pic, aw-shucks Owen Wilson borne back against the currents of

time, learning as only a naive American can that all paradises are lost or that they never existed.

The prototypical homesick person was Homer's Odysseus, cast up on Kalypso's Ogygia and yearning for Ithaka. When we meet him, in book 5 of the *Odyssey*, he is gazing out at the sea, crying for wife and home, for a person and a place. Odysseus makes it back, of course. (So does Agamemnon, but with disastrous consequences.) Ruth, in the Old Testament, is also a mythical exile, but as a literary figure she is most touchingly rendered by Keats in "Ode to a Nightingale": "Through the sad heart of Ruth, when, sick for home, / She stood in tears amid the alien corn." There is no biblical authority for this portrayal. Keats, born after the invention of the word, makes "nostalgia" an appropriate condition for his sad gleaner. The original Ruth would not have known the meaning of the word, even in her desire for the land of her Moabite tribesmen. Exile and displacement are eternal; nostalgia is a modern phenomenon, not a biblical one. Keats's Ruth has a romantic disease.

Other nostalgias direct us not to specific places, or even to people except secondarily, but to a time, to the past. We long for our youth, which Robert Schumann depicted musically in *Kinderszenen*, his piano suite originally called *Leichte Stücke*, "easy pieces." Schumann then changed his mind, and his title, when he realized that neither the pieces themselves nor the period to which they referred were as easy as we sometimes pretend.

Music is the perfect conveyor of nostalgia. Composers can resolve their chords, offer lulling harmonies; performers can soothe us gently. Ned Rorem once suggested provocatively that music makes us nostalgic for the future; that is, it makes us look forward to auditory resolutions. Music makes us cry. The visual arts seldom do this, if only because language, like sound in general, has a stronger hold on our deepest feelings than objects we see. Nostalgia means melancholy without pain, a penumbra of chronic, thoughtless homesickness, a bland watercolor wash of feelings, or a bittersweet longing for auld lang syne that might not have been so good in actuality. Think of the weepy parlor songs on either side of the so-called Gay Nineties that evoke distant times and places ("On the Banks of the Wabash, Far Away," "When You and I Were Young, Maggie," "School Days," practically anything by Stephen Foster), or even—continuing with music—those sentimental twentieth-century songs that anticipate a better future, in tunes that to today's ears sound quaintly sweet, even though the words themselves may prefigure or intimate tragedy. Think of songs from World War I ("Till We Meet Again") and World War II ("We'll Meet Again"), whose virtually identical titles match their virtually identical sentiments. Death is not mentioned. The boys marched off to war; many did not return. The music allows us to remember the pieties and harmonies of what we idealize as simpler times. Cheerful tones mask the likelihood of destruction.

What Norman Rockwell and Currier & Ives are to pictorial nostalgia, Samuel Barber's *Knoxville: Summer of 1915* is to musical nostalgia. James Agee wrote his gentle reminiscence of childhood in 1938. Barber's musical setting came a decade later. The two men, born within four months of each other, were five in 1915. Both the words and the music had almost spontaneous compositions, or at least both men worked with ease and relative speed. Agee said he wrote his piece in ninety minutes. Both the lulling words and music, the evocation of small-town America (a southern version of Grover's Corners or Bedford Falls, even Mark Twain's Hannibal, Missouri), and the aura of safety, with a child falling to sleep and protected by warm weather and warm relatives, represent the quintessential American dream of a benign past. Barber composed his piece in 1947. The world had just come through a catastrophic decade.

Scenes of childhood and adolescence invariably involve other people unless one grew up in unfriendly isolation. We think of those we shared our time with, especially as life itself becomes, chillingly, shorter with each passing day. We know what our end will be. We sense the sands moving more swiftly through the hourglass. If it was happy, the past offers at least the luxury of solace. In the past, we had a future. In the present, as we age, we have mostly a past. Remembering when we had a future gives any senior citizen a core for his nostalgia. The past will not abandon us. We can hold on to it. As Bogart says to Bergman in *Casablanca*, "We'll always have Paris."

You can go home again, at least to a place—whether Ithaka or a childhood manse—but you cannot go back in time, except in memory, or accidental encounters with old friends, or those occasional moments of high-spirited jollity, planned but not imposed. I am thinking of class reunions. What impels people to go to them—high school, college—those famous "gaudies" celebrated by Dorothy Sayers and other clubbable Brits, or the more democratic, back-patting old-boy-old-girl networking of an American version? I count myself among the guilty. Or the lucky. At the tenth, old sores may still ooze, old animosities still simmer, and old flames may burn. At the twenty-fifth, one has, ideally, reached maturity with a judicious combination of contentment and compromise. One vivacious younger friend told me that she compelled her husband, tall, dark, handsome, and very successful, to come with her to her twenty-fifth high school reunion because, as she put it, "I had major scores to settle. I wanted to show them that I wasn't just a brain." This woman is a distinguished academic with impeccable feminist credentials, at least in theory if not entirely in practice. The trophy husband complied, not happily.

At the fiftieth, no one cares or asks "What do you do?" They don't even give your partner the once-over. "How are you?" replaces "What are you?" We are more interested in someone's health than in his status and accomplishments. Voltaire wisely remarked that after eighty all contemporaries are friends. They know where they are going, and they are going there both alone and together.

I was looking forward to my fiftieth high school reunion, but now I can't quite figure out why. Like Updike, I had always thought long and hard, and with a smile, about classmates from early childhood and adolescence. I remembered most of them fondly, even the ones who might have scared or annoyed me when I was a know-it-all baby beatnik, a pesky intellectual who resisted football games, pep rallies, anything that smacked of mindless conformity. These kids gave me a good part of my education. I did not know this at the time it was happening. Looking back can be instructive.

My friend Paula Marantz Cohen, ten years my junior, had a similar anxiety about her fortieth reunion in central New Jersey: "I got into the spirit myself, which I would never have done in high school, where not getting into the spirit of anything had been one of the salient aspects of my profile." Her big event turned out to be more successful than mine. Or, rather, she had better results. Does this say something about her or about the event? About both, of course.

My reunion, like hers, had been impeccably organized by a bunch of stalwart classmates with energy, goodwill, and hope. Vestigial school spirit and fellow feeling, as well as common courtesy, prevailed. There we were in suburban Philadelphia, 120 of the original 468 of us, plus an appropriate number of willing spouses and partners, those disposed to spend an evening with scores of people they had never met and would probably never see again. Wiser or less tolerant partners stayed home. ("Not tonight, dear; please go alone," I can hear them pleading or asserting.) Fifteen percent of us had already died; another 10 percent were unreachable for more mundane reasons. A bit more than 25 percent made it to the country club. Some of the enthusiastic organizers assured me that this is a good percentage for big public high schools. Only private schools, or otherwise small and intimate ones, do better.

Who were we? We had as our common bond age and a shared history. Growing up in suburban Philadelphia, the first postwar babies, we were the children of the ballyhooed "greatest generation," the men and women who came to maturity during the Depression, who endured the "good war" and then settled down. Cultural historians used to condemn the Eisenhower years as the decade of complacent conformity. Those years are now undergoing an upward revaluation, as is Eisenhower himself, because America could boast both a solid middle class and a steady, growing economy. We grew up accompanied by television, the civil rights movement, early Elvis, and the incandescence of Kennedy's Camelot before the date that changed everything—November 22, 1963—and before Vietnam, hippies, drugs, and the burning of American cities.

"Bliss was it in that dawn to be alive," wrote Wordsworth, looking back to a comparable period, before the idealism of the French Revolution turned bloody, "but to be young was very heaven." We—middle-class, almost exclusively white, largely Jewish—could say the same thing. Even more than most young people, we had optimism on our side, in the water we drank and the air we breathed. This same optimism must have accounted for a disproportionate percentage of Jewish classmates who helped to plan, and who attended, the reunion. We were the inheritors of the label *am ha-sefer,* "the people of the book," and in most cases we were only one to three generations removed from immigrant status. Our ancestors had made the trip from shtetl to suburb with amazing speed. Education—what it promised, what it meant, and what it delivered—was of the greatest importance to us, the secularized descendants of old-world forebears, most of whom were more religious than we. It is no false nostalgia to say that regardless of normal hormonal challenges and exertions, our coming-of-age was easy compared with what today's high school students undergo. We had no metal detectors in the school doorways, because we had no guns, no knives. Violence did not exist except on the football field. We had neither cyber bullying nor too much of the old-fashioned physical kind. The biggest misdemeanors: cutting class and smoking cigarettes in the bathrooms. I look back accurately, not only with eyes dimmed by sentiment.

Those who showed up would probably agree with my recollections and assessments. But what of the absentees? People stay away from imposed collective nostalgia for many reasons: shame, or at least embarrassment; fear of reopening the old wounds; pervasive lack of interest in the past. Not everyone shared my genial fondness for the whole, imagined group of us. Many classmates loomed large in my memory, in smile-inducing ways, just as Updike's Shillington schoolmates did in his. I wrote notes, made phone calls. "I'm going to the reunion; will I see you there?" They demurred. They had no interest in the class soiree. "I hated high school," said one, a class officer, an athlete, a golden boy. Another, a silver-tongued lawyer, confessed, "I'll have nothing to say." My invitation got me nowhere. They would be happy to see me, they said, but certainly not at the country club, not at this event. They maintained sangfroid invisibility. I shall have to schedule a private appointment.

One friend made it in from London. She has spent most of her life abroad as a middle school teacher, and she took a characteristically clear-eyed view of the whole event: "The reunion taught me a lot. I learned that the people I disliked in high school I still disliked, and the people I liked were still good. And I finally understood what happened in junior high, where I spent the rest of my life. And I learned that [...] has not changed. And I missed [...]. And I can't imagine what life would have been like if we had stuck around the Philly burbs for the last fifty years."

Many of my classmates had in fact stuck around. No surprise: most people still live within a radius of several zip codes from where they have always lived. Some of my contemporaries have moved across the Delaware River to southern New Jersey, which is really another suburb of Philadelphia. A large number have relocated to Florida, which qualifies as an extension of the Northeast.

I learned another lesson. Some people look back with disinterest or no interest; with nothing to feel ashamed of, they still put the past aside. And many people simply prefer not to look back. They are moving on to the next thing, whatever that may be. They don't have to look back. They have something to look forward to. Perhaps the most daring of us, however happy our adolescence might have been, do not require the balm provided by nostalgia.

We gathered—achievers, retirees, grandparents, the married, the widowed, the divorced, the always single—in a predictable array of bodies and outfits. We are doctors, lawyers, educators, businesspeople, scientists, bankers, engineers, health spa owners, air-conditioning repairmen, policemen, factory workers, and women who have never worked outside the home: a well-filled cornucopia of middle-class American success. Physical health, financial security, and ample preservation prevailed among the attendees, with some predictable exceptions: a cheerleader turned roly-poly, a star athlete confined to a wheelchair, another former Adonis walking with a cane in the early stages of Parkinson's disease. Are they the same, or not the same, as they once were? How do you feel when you confront life's depredations made visible? In the eye of the beholder, pity competes with schadenfreude.

At the end of *À la recherche du temps perdu*, Proust's narrator, Marcel, attends a soiree at the home of the formidable princesse de Guermantes, where he finds the relics of his past, the characters of the whole novel, the beauties now wizened, the strong weakened, the upright bent, the raven-haired gone white or bald. Of a woman he remembers as a young girl, he observes, "This nose, this new nose of hers, opened up horizons of possibilities one would have never dared hope for. Kindness and tender affection, formerly out of the question, became possible with those cheeks. One could make clear to a person with that chin things one would never have thought attempting with the possessor of the previous one" (I'm using the old Frederick A. Blossom translation). Marcel is not referring to plastic surgery here. Today, he might very well be confronted with it. I certainly was at my reunion. Science and cosmetics had worked noticeable wonders. Some of the women looked finer, leaner, and more beautiful than they had been at eighteen. Time takes away, but it also sustains and, with a little help, improves us. What Marcel thought lost he has refound. And Proust's tone—a little arch, a little wistful, a little hyperbolic—suggests different registers of feeling when one confronts the past.

The question is, what does it mean to "recognize" someone? Marcel notices what he calls "the geology of a face," with its creases, erosions, deposits, and layers: a series of selves like the pentimenti of a painting. Some people, instantly recognizable, "as though in harmonious agreement with the season, adopted gray hair as their personal adornment for the autumn." Nature and artifice can work together with splendid results. Different kinds of surprises await us when we enter a room prepared for a renewal of scenes of childhood. The duc de Guermantes shows his age—eighty-three!—relatively little until he tries to stand up and totters "on trembling limbs." And Marcel contemplates stasis and change, those two staples of every human life, and how we remain the same under or over, beyond or in spite of, the evidence of difference. He realizes that one starts out with the idea "that people have remained the same and one finds them old. But once one starts out with the idea that they are old, one finds them much as they used to be, not looking so badly after all." In other words, change your focus, readjust the mental image, and the former person—the old friend—reappears now, when actually old, as the same as when you knew him. Marcel says of one such rediscovery, "For me, who had known him at the threshold of life, he was still my young companion, a youth whose age I calculated from the age which I consciously assigned to myself under the impression that I had not grown any older since that time."

Everyone has versions of these revelations. Several years ago, I made a breakfast date with a friend, unseen for forty years, when we both found ourselves in the same small New England town one summer weekend. Partners were not invited: it was to be the two of us, old high school cronies. As usual, I was early. I stood on the sidewalk and looked at the women passing by. Could this one be Sue? Unlikely. What about that one? Too tall. Another? Too blond. And so it went. I was about to approach one less unlikely candidate when suddenly I turned from my right to my left and my friend hove into view. "Hello, Sue," I said, grateful for my patience and astuteness and even more for her unchangingness. She looked just like herself, even a bit more so.

But the opposite also happens. Someone came up to me at the reunion and said, "Remember me?" He wore no name tag. How could I remember this man, who bore no resemblance to anyone I had ever seen? He had made an egregious faux pas that common sense should have prevented. Never assume that anyone knows who you are. The secret to polite inquiry, of course, is to make the first move and introduce, that is, reintroduce yourself: "Hello, Willard. I'm David Smith. Do you remember me?"

To which the correct answer is, "David, of course. You haven't changed. How are you?" Never give the other person a chance to embarrass both of you. Take the initiative. But do not assume that all is the same or that time has not passed. The addressee picks up the challenge and maintains the fiction that you are still hail-fellows-well-met, easily and cheerfully recognized. Let your viewer slowly examine your face, body, and voice, to attempt an act of archaeological recovery. Yes, there's something about the mouth, or the jaw, or the cock of the head, the accent, or even the dimple: why, it's David, of course. Proust was, again, right when he observed that "the beauty of an object is to be found behind the object—that of an idea, in front of it."

With age, some people seem to lose all of their bad qualities, others to heighten their good ones. These are the fortunate ones. This is true of both body and—more infrequently—temperament or soul. Some people become nicer. The edge wears off. Adolescent hormones evaporated decades before. At my party, some of the class clowns seemed less self-assertive. They had slowed down.

Humanity often reasserts itself when and where we might least expect it to do so. People become more themselves, but they also transform themselves.

At the age of twenty-one, young John Keats knew many truths, scientific, psychological, and emotional. Among them is this one, articulated in a letter:

> Our bodies every seven years are completely fresh-materiald— seven years ago it was not this hand that clench'd itself against Hammond—We are like the relict garments of a Saint: the same and not the same: for the careful Monks patch it and patch it: till there's not a thread of the original garment left, and still they show it for St. Anthony's shirt. This is the reason why men who had been bosom friends, on being separated for any number of years, afterwards meet coldly, neither of them knowing why—The fact is they are both altered—Men who live together have a silent moulding and influencing power over each other—They inter-assimilate. 'Tis an uneasy thought that in seven years the same hands cannot greet each other again. All this may be obviated by a willful and dramatic exercise of our Minds towards each other.

But the same hands can and do greet each other. When we make that willful and dramatic exercise of the mind, when we direct it to others in a rush of bonhomie, we are acknowledging the steady constancy beneath the appearance of change. Had Keats lived more than his fully packed twenty-five years, would he have accepted the truth of Yeats's "Among School Children," namely, that we change without knowing it? We all look at ourselves every day in the mirror, washing, shaving, combing hair, and putting on makeup, and every morning we always look the same. Then we see a photograph, or are trapped in the unflattering glare of a dressing room's three-way mirror, and we are stopped in our tracks: "When did I become old?" We are the same, and not the same. We all had pretty plumage once, or, as an astute friend of mine once observed, you spend the first half of your life wishing you looked like someone else and the second half of your life wishing you looked like yourself in the first half of that life. We experience our life as continuity, not as separate steps; we confront radical change in others.

Our class reunion party was not aristocratic, not even grand. It was democratic and claustrophobic. No one could make an entrance: this was suburban Philadelphia, not a Paris salon. People just floated in at the cocktail hour, milled about, had dinner, stayed for dancing, or left after dessert. Hierarchy did not exist. After all, this was America. Casualness, not precision, prevailed. Did I achieve anything like an epiphany at the country club on that brisk, calm autumn evening? Did I learn anything? Was I struck dumb? Alas, no: I had no revelations, heard no confessions, no admissions of former passion, and no apologies for slights or wrongs from the past. The event was as modestly pleasurable, even banal, as it could have been. That I probably won't see most of these people ever again—despite several lame jokes about our seventy-fifth reunion—neither saddened me nor made the shared pleasantries any sharper. Had I missed the event to begin with, I would have lost out on nothing except cordiality and some fine dancing to the music we grew up with: swing, cha-cha, a little Chubby Checker twisting for the really risqué. Anticipation of the event led to a subsequent letdown.

One friend flew up from Florida with some curiosity but few expectations. She had a lovely time, she told me afterward, because she had no previous ideas or hopes. I realized that this is a good way to go through life: expect nothing and you will never be disenchanted, only agreeably surprised. I had so resolutely planned on an outpouring of fine feeling that I had set myself up for disappointment. Instead of the longed-for inundation came a modest wash of sentiments and the sweet frustration of conversations nipped in the bud, which are always preferable to ones that go on too long. Thank goodness for the easy out—"I think I'll have another drink," "I must say hello to my former next-door neighbor," or "Oh, look, there's Diane"—to keep alive what Wallace Stevens called the pleasures of merely circulating.

Most of the old differences among us had melted away, in favor of an acknowledgment of our commonalities. We have led—everyone does—generic lives. Everyone had work and love, Freud's two great conditions, to talk about, although successes and failures alike both took a backseat to more mundane topics ("What is the weather like in Florida?" "How is your golf game?" "You have how many grandchildren?") and, only fleetingly, more prodding or spiritual ones. Deep conversation, analysis, and intimacy were in short supply; fellow feeling and high spirits prevailed. These offered disappointments as well as pleasure. But what was I thinking? Did I really expect that old obsessions would reappear, old flames burst out? Did I expect confessions, revelations, and admissions? The people I had crushes on fifty years past did not show up. What would I have done had they appeared? I wanted to have experiences at the country club that would have been worth replaying and reviewing, just as I wanted to replay and review experiences from half a century before with the cast of characters from the play called "My Life." It is probably just as well that nothing memorable occurred.

D. H. Lawrence begins his poem "Beautiful Old Age" with a conditional verb: "It ought to be lovely to be old / to be full of the peace that comes of experience / and wrinkled ripe fulfilment." Lawrence died at forty-four, well before he could experience the final ripening and rotting. He might have known an 1827 poem by Wordsworth that begins, "Such age how beautiful!" ("To ——, in Her Seventeenth Year"). Only a special person would say this. By "special," I do not mean merely "a poet," but a poet of a certain age, one who, like Wordsworth, born in 1770, is approaching, but not entirely close to, the age of his addressee. This is what the future holds, if luck, genetics, and healthy living can keep body and spirit together and sustain us. Wordsworth must have projected himself into the Countess of X, looking at his future state in her present one. Anyone over fifty knows the feeling. We see ourselves in others, and especially in the old we find our mirrored selves. Even the gods become ghosts.

As you get older, you become more sensitive to the ravages of age and more grateful for the occasional evidence that not everyone deteriorates terribly. Some people look much better. Others at least change interestingly. A while ago, I ran into a man I know slightly. He's six years younger than I, gray-haired, straight spined, handsomely preserved. When I met him for the first time at a dinner party several years earlier, I blurted out, "Have you ever been a model?" To which the answer was yes. Now, at sixty-one, the bone structure is still there; the body is intact. Whatever indignities age has visited upon him—arthritis, knee replacement—do not show immediately. Instead, you find the traces of youthful beauty, the past recaptured or still in evidence, and also a deepening of that beauty. I think of Wordsworth, in "Tintern Abbey": "for such loss, I would believe, / Abundant recompense." Wordsworth was twenty-eight when he wrote this. What form exactly does that recompense take? Does wisdom come out of bodily decrepitude? Perhaps, but everyone remains excited by bodily beauty, especially when his own body has lost strength and resiliency. We remain nostalgic for our former, sexually charged selves. What can you do to work with the hand nature has dealt you?

My less than overwhelming experience—Proust goes to the country club—came several months ahead of another trip, this one to Mexico to visit friends for a long weekend. The place and the company were congenial, the weather perfect. The visit was filled with chat in several languages, music and museums, dancing on the plaza. On a Monday, I prepared for my return to Dallas.

Maybe because I was born two weeks premature, I have an almost constitutional capacity and instinct for earliness. I always get to airports well before I need to, eager for what will follow. I like airports almost as much as I like travel. Many friends call my taste for both the terminal and the plane inexplicable if not bizarre, although discomfort is the price one pays for whatever pleasures await at the destination, the next place. To go somewhere, you must endure the voyage. I have never minded it. T. S. Eliot was again right: "The journey not the arrival matters."

And then I realized: I like to look forward as much as backward. I am like those friends who didn't come to the reunion because they prefer not to look back. Something ahead always invites us. Which has greater vividness, the past or the future? I sit in an airport waiting room, impatient. I sit on the plane itself in heightened anticipation, perhaps more than a little tense. My antennae are on the alert. My body and mind are primed: Something is going to happen! In that waiting room and on that plane, we passengers are all pilgrims together. There is no disappointment. Once in the air, we are literally suspended, going between. And the community of travelers, however temporary, is one of equals. There's no us, no them, no natives, no foreigners. No one belongs and everyone does. No hierarchy. Even first-class passengers do not reach the goal any faster. They may have better seats and more legroom; they may enjoy free warm nuts and champagne, but midair turbulence does not spare them. And if there's a delay, we are all delayed. Blandness and banality confer their own comfort. In a foreign country, you tend to be ill at ease in the unfamiliar. In the waiting room, you inhabit a state of betweenness, as you do in midair. In the waiting room, you're not even traveling, you are just sitting or pacing, recovering from where you have been, anticipating where you are heading, whether home or away from it. You are powerfully aware of your status, actual and symbolic, in present time. And you are looking ahead. Lacking the normal ballast of familiar circumstances—all the aspects of our daily life that make us forget we have little control over our destiny—you may also feel the shock of any journey, knowing all too well where all journeys take us.

This time, I—we—waited for the arrival of the little plane that would return us to the States. The plane kept not coming. The first announcement said, simply, "Weather." Then another announcement said, "Mechanical malfunction." We kept waiting. Finally, we were all asked to spend the night at the local Holiday Inn and to get ready for a return flight at five the next morning. Fellow passengers grabbed their phones to contact friends and relatives on the other side. Grumbles, groans, modest gnashing of teeth, some cursing, were heard. There was nothing to be done.

We gathered in the hotel bar and restaurant, thirty-five of us, all going nowhere, and settled in for an evening of modest, obligatory solidarity, the sharing of personal details, and having another drink. We smiled and laughed. We got to know one another. We became a community of circumstance and convenience. We went to bed, awoke in the middle of the night, returned to the little airport, and came home. The intimacies of the previous night had vanished like a dream. Now each of us was grimly set on a return to the practicalities of ordinary civilian life. We looked forward.

I thought of another man getting ready to set out. Herodotus tells the story of Xerxes, surveying his troops, thousands of men, the pride of the Persian Empire, as they prepared to cross the Hellespont to invade Greece, ca. 480 B.C.E. The emperor overlooked his vast expeditionary force—plumes flying, armor glinting, beautiful men eager for warfare and glory—and he remarked with sadness, "Look at all these people—but not one of them will be alive in a hundred years." His estimate was too generous, of course. Surely most of the men had died within half the allotted, predicted time.

My big high school reunion flew by quickly: four hours of socializing. It was as cheerful as it was brief, if nothing special. It offered little by way of lightning flashes or thunder rolls. And then it came to me: it was like life itself, miniaturized. Edna St. Vincent Millay, who knew about the speed at which, say, a candle burns, knew both the truth of our inevitable disappearance and the opposing urge not to give in:

> Down, down, down into the darkness of the grave
> Gently they go, the beautiful, the tender, the kind;
> Quietly they go, the intelligent, the witty, the brave.
> I know. But I do not approve. And I am not resigned.
> ("Dirge Without Music")

It all went by, and it continues to go by, so fast. Proust has it right in the last sentence of his novel: time itself is a place, "extending boundlessly . . . giant-like, reaching back into the years," in which we can "touch simultaneously epochs of [our] lives—with countless intervening days between—so widely separated from another in Time."

Life eventually becomes for everyone "drear and deadly" as Updike put it, but for some—most? the lucky few?—it offers gratification as well. Looking back becomes itself a source of such pleasure. Looking forward tests one's strength and hope. Wordsworth said, famously, in his Intimations Ode that a mature person finds "strength in what remains behind." The phrasing suggests, ambiguously, that we are grateful for what strength remains within us after much has been taken and also that we continue, unavoidably, to look back, "behind" us, to identify and relish the source of that strength.

QUIET ✒

Many writers have been making a lot of noise about silence during the past few years, all of them "listening" in order to hear something, or "confronting" and "pursuing" in an effort to achieve some kind of escape. The virtually interchangeable titles of their books ring changes on one common theme. This is literature by people on an impossible mission, a quest unlikely to be fulfilled.

I have read many of these articulations of the last decade. More will come forth as more people feel the need to weigh in with their opinions and experiences. Stuart Sim has written a *Manifesto for Silence: Confronting the Politics and Culture of Noise* (2007). Anne D. LeClaire, in *Listening Below the Noise: A Meditation on the Practice of Silence* (2009), describes her decision—and its consequences—not to speak for an entire Monday. One day of silence turned into two Mondays every month for seventeen years; her experiment included a week on Cape Cod with no speech and no electronic sounds whatsoever. In 2010, George Prochnik (*In Pursuit of Silence: Listening for Meaning in a World of Noise*) ventured into, among other subjects, the sociology of noise in shopping malls; the creation of antinoise societies in England and America starting in the early twentieth century; "deaf architecture" at Gallaudet University and elsewhere; the physiology of sound; and the history of soundproofing. In *Listening to Noise and Silence: Towards a Philosophy of Sound Art* (2010), Salomé Voegelin makes a more abstract philosophical effort "to consider listening as an actual practice and as a conceptual sensibility." Most interesting, Sara Maitland, in *A Book of Silence* (2008), a book succinctly titled and lacking the requisite academic colon, writes autobiographically about her gradual moving away from a noisy, intellectual, upper-class but bohemian British family, through the early days of feminism, to falling in love with silence and solitude. She hung out with Bill Clinton in the heady, turbulent Oxford of the late 1960s and then abandoned the clamor of public political and philosophical debate for marriage and child rearing and finally for the solace of private spirituality.

The same obsession has haunted the newspapers as well. People are looking for old-fashioned peace and quiet, and they find it in both old and new ways. Some people, like LeClaire, just stop talking. Others simply turn off phones, computers, and the other antennae that connect them to the noisy world outside. I have kept clippings of articles from *The New York Times* about this obsession in an ever-expanding folder. They include pieces by, for example, Susan Gregory Thomas, writing in the travel section (2012), looking for "a quick shot of peace, on a budget," and recommending various inexpensive spiritual venues where one might find "no-frills spiritual solitude." She found hers at a Jesuit center in Pennsylvania. In the Book Review, John Plotz wrote an essay on the "noonday demons" that afflicted medieval monks and the modern incarnations of such demons. Plotz visited a Benedictine monastery in central Massachusetts in his quest for communal solitude and quiet. Maureen Dowd, in an Op-Ed piece from 2011, quotes the twentieth-century Swiss philosopher Max Picard: "Nothing has changed the nature of man so much as the loss of silence." Susan Cain, author of the bestselling 2012 book *Quiet: The Power of Introverts in a World That Can't Stop Talking,* wrote a *Times* piece before her book came out. It begins, "Solitude is out of fashion."

Most moving was a 2012 piece by Pico Iyer called "The Joy of Quiet," which reminds us that the average American spends eight and a half hours a day in front of a screen; that the average office worker has no more than three minutes at a time without interruption; that you can now spend lots of money at "black-hole resorts," where you pay for the privilege of not having a television in your room. This is the equivalent of spending lots of money for a week at a spa where you get healthful but very minimal food. The more you pay, the less you eat. Today, several years after Iyer's article, the data must be even more staggering. Like other writers, Iyer has been going on retreat for decades. His preferred destination is a Benedictine hermitage in California. While in residence, he does not attend services; he does not meditate. He merely walks and reads. You do not need to go to a monastery to do these things. You could just as easily stay home, but perhaps the temptations to succumb to worldly distractions are too great. Iyer quotes the fashionable designer Philippe Starck, who claims, "I never read any magazines or watch TV. Nor do I go to cocktail parties, dinners, or anything like that." Anyone can live like this.

But it has always been thus. Some people work best alone and in quiet. Many people, especially writers, seek out the condition of solitude and its mate, tranquillity. The immediate precursors of the current generation of mindful silence seekers include Annie Dillard, Patrick Leigh Fermor, Peter Francis, Anne Morrow Lindbergh, Thomas Merton, Kathleen Norris, and Picard and, before them, generations of secular as well as religious men and women who wanted calm instead of fury. People have always put their fingers in their ears or walked out of a room in their search for quiet. Google

"noise" and you find—by my latest count—forty-one million en-
tries. Google "silence" and you turn up only twenty-eight million.
And writers talk—that is, write—about silence endlessly. Justice
Oliver Wendell Holmes recommended silence as a cure "for the
blows of sound." Aldous Huxley called noise "an assault against silence." George Bernard Shaw said with tongue in cheek, "I believe
in the discipline of silence and could talk for hours about it." Probably a minute after God created the world with language ("Let
there be light"; and "In the beginning was the Word, and the Word
was with God and the Word was God"), someone said "Shhhh" or
"Can you please turn it down?" Someone has always complained to
someone else about the noise, either unwanted human speech or
harsh, loud nonhuman sounds coming from elsewhere.

Everything is relative. I think of Ernest Thesiger's campy reply
to someone asking about his experience at the Battle of the Somme
in World War I: "Oh, my dear. The noise! And the people!" Or W. C.
Fields, having been offered a Bromo-Seltzer for a hangover by a
solicitous waiter: "Ye Gods, no! I couldn't stand the noise."

There is, of course, no such thing as "noise," just as—in the
famous words of John Cage recalling the 1952 premiere of
4′33″,—"there's no such thing as silence." A noise is merely a sound
that you happen not to like or a decibel level that you find oppressive. Just as a weed is not a thing in nature but only a plant rooted
where someone doesn't want it, so one man's noise can be another
man's music. When Julia Barnett Rice, a New York grande dame
whom the Parisian press dubbed "the Queen of Silence," founded
the Society for the Suppression of Unnecessary Noise in 1906, her
particular bête noire was Hudson River tugboats that disturbed
her sleep. Today many people might find the call of the river tug-
boat, like a train whistle in the night, a source of comfortably sopo-
rific nostalgic pleasure.

On her visits downtown, Mrs. Rice turned up her nose and
plugged her ears, calling the Lower East Side "the saddest place,"

with the "unnecessary rackets" of its pushcarts, the same carts that Lorenz Hart heard as "gliding by" sweetly on Mott Street ("Manhattan"). This was not the charming shtetl depicted in *Funny Girl*, Jule Styne and Bob Merrill's musical about plucky Fanny Brice rising from poverty to stardom, or the dense, teeming neighborhood remembered more realistically but appreciatively in Irving Howe's *World of Our Fathers*. Slums, ghettos, shtetls, have always been subjects for analysis and nostalgia equally, and fond backward glances compete with hardheaded evaluations of the realities of life. John Connell, a British civil servant, started the Noise Abatement Society in the United Kingdom, which led to the 1960 Noise Abatement Act that tried to regulate noise from burglar alarms. Today we also have car alarms. Whatever measures we take to lower the din, nothing seems to help. And what offends one person, or an entire generation, another person or generation may simply ignore. There is no getting away from the perils of noise.

Unless you are deaf, total silence is not a possibility. In this, it differs from darkness, which under the right circumstances you can experience. Several years ago, I traveled through the Blue Ridge Mountains of Virginia, a region filled with caves that anyone can visit. It was a rainy, gray January weekday morning. Summer tourists, kids on school trips, and almost all other potential visitors had disappeared. I stopped at Endless Caverns. Nine people gathered at the ticket booth, and an amiable guide led us on our descent. Like Dante going down into the underworld, we stepped carefully, not so much fearful as modestly anxious. More than a hundred feet beneath the earth's surface, our soft-spoken guide told us to circle around and to hold on to one another. "You will now experience total darkness," she said, and flipped a light switch that plunged us all into blackness so deep that I could not see a hand in front of my face. Or anything else. We stood this way for no more than two terrifying minutes, and then the light returned, relieving our anxiety. A bit shaken, we climbed back up to the cave's mouth and welcomed the day, which—however damp, dreary, and full of gloom—seemed spectacularly sunny.

How often one wishes for that final or Platonic pair of earplugs that will eliminate all sounds, pleasant as well as noxious, appreciated as well as unwanted, necessary as well as superfluous. To do this would require strenuous measures, possible only in a specially equipped sensory-deprivation laboratory. And people have tried for a long time to get the desired results. Thomas Carlyle fantasized about a soundproof room; Franz Kafka ordered his earplugs from Berlin, imagining that the technicians in a big sophisticated city could provide him with greater comfort than what he had available to him in provincial Prague. More recently, one wealthy, eccentric, and phonophobic New Yorker commissioned an architect to build for him the world's quietest house on Long Island, but he then complained that he could hear the front door and then the hum of something in his desk.

As silence gets closer, we hear smaller things, like our computer's tiny motor. Even the fanciest equipment can do only so much to reduce, let alone eliminate, the ambient noise. The equivalent of my underground spelunking blackness would be an anechoic chamber, which can go down to −10 decibels. (For comparison, a jet engine is 150 decibels; a jackhammer 100 decibels; a very calm room 20–30 decibels.) You can achieve a partial effect with noise-canceling headphones, but these never do the whole job. In an airplane, you can blot out nearby conversations, but you still hear the thrum of the jet engines. And even if total noise elimination were possible, one's body produces internal vibrations, transmitted through the bones and corporeal fluids; in the absence of external sound, you will hear your own self, first your heart and then the blood moving through it.

I have been thinking about sound and noise, quiet and silence, and the inadequacy of speech—the very words we use to talk about sound—for a while. It is not mere curmudgeonhood that accounts for one's increasing intolerance for certain kinds of noise. Everyone, especially over a certain age, can make a list of pet peeves: the cell phone going off inopportunely in the concert hall; loud conversations in railway cars; the constant presence of televisions in airports; rap music blaring from open car windows on city streets; the howling of a dog that has been cooped up all day at home in the adjacent apartment; restaurants in which civilized conversation is no longer possible; the low moan of a neighbor's "entertainment center"; or the tapping of stiletto heels on a bare floor in the apartment above you. Some people cover their ears when a subway car or fire truck screeches by; the screechiness, like chalk on a blackboard, even more than the volume, offends them. Others are more disturbed by human sounds—wailing babies, sparring domestic partners—than industrial and mechanical ones. Many of us wince more when, traveling abroad, we hear our compatriots hollering en masse than when we hear the similarly loud sounds coming from people of other nationalities or in languages we do not understand. We make allowances for others. We forgive the foreigner, but shrill cries in English raise the blood pressure.

And thank goodness for the so-called Quiet Cars on Amtrak.

What deafens one person's ears and deadens the spirit gives pleasure and uplift to someone else. Consider the generous, sympathetic, worldly toleration of Jane Austen's narrator in *Persuasion*:

> Everybody has their taste in noises as well as in other matters; and sounds are quite innoxious or most distressing, by their sort rather than their quantity. When Lady Russell, not long afterwards, was entering Bath on a wet afternoon, and driving through the long course of streets from the Old Bridge to Camden Place, amidst the dash of other carriages, the heavy rumble of carts and drays, the bawling of newsmen, muffin-men, and milkmen, and the ceaseless clink of pattens, she made no complaint. No, these

were noises which belonged to the winter pleasures; her spirits
rose under their influence.

More than any of her other novels, *Persuasion* radiates with Austen's
warm appreciation of human difference in tastes, habits, and predi-
lections. Everyone loves his or her own ways best, and Austen
reminds us that these preferences are like aesthetic choices—felt
along the pulse, in the body as well as the spirit—and infinitely
expandable. Her wisdom is not mere feel-good cultural relativism
but intelligent, pragmatic hedonism that encourages us to tolerate
one another for the sake of civic harmony.

Responses to sound change with age. Many babies can sleep
through an explosion. Most adults cannot. Our responses change,
as well, with location. Consider music. Noise can hold us captive in
the concert hall. On the radio or stereo, we can adjust the volume,
minimize discordancy, put obtrusive sounds into a background
buzz. But it is also a well-acknowledged truth that people who tolerate or even relish chic radical experiments in the visual arts are
usually much slower to accept the latest experiments in music. In a
museum, you can walk past something that doesn't appeal to you.
An art historian friend of mine talks about "noisy paintings," echoing Diderot, the *encyclopédiste* who said that Boucher's pictures create
"an unbearable racket for the eye." Still, you can simply shut your
eyes or avert your glance when you see something that bores or offends you. (Three centuries ago, Richard Steele made a similar observation and lodged the same complaint: "I have often lamented
that we cannot close our ears with as much ease as we can our eyes.")
In the concert hall, you sit imprisoned by both dissonant sounds
and the length of time required to endure them. A person can be
tortured through sound but not, for the most part, through sight.

Silence, like the star-studded nighttime sky formerly available
to all but now invisible to virtually everyone, has become a lost
commodity. Some of us make efforts to retrieve it. Privacy and

slowness, equally in short supply, are its cousins, requiring cultiva-
tion. Noise, like public life and communal activity, dissipates as well
as stimulates energy. Thoreau had it right: "Silence is the universal
refuge, the sequel to all dull discourses and all foolish acts." Where
do we, especially those of us who live in cities, find it? Do we really
need CNN in airports or music in restaurants? Without entering a
Trappist monastery, or otherwise taking a vow of silence, how can
we effect noise reduction in our daily lives? If you have the good
fortune to live on a vast property, you may have momentary respite.
But few people can, or wish to, remain agoraphobic forever. We live
in the world. Nature—a park, a lake, a desert, even a backyard—
can offer weekend solace, although the hum if not the roar of traffic,
the most pervasive noise on the planet, exists everywhere, in the
country as well as the metropolis.

Silence has a next of kin, however: it is called Quiet. We can try
to discover or achieve, and then maintain it, sometimes with difficulty. For years, I have looked for tranquillity in four kinds of urban
venues. You used to be able to eat a civilized meal in an intimate
restaurant and enjoy serious conversations in hushed tones. When I
was in college, long ago and far away, we would drive to New York
from the provinces to enjoy big-city delights: museums, concerts,
plays, and, most of all, food. Too much mystery meat, covered
with bland brown gravy, from the university cafeteria can turn a
desperate, hungry adolescent into a budding epicure in search of
a more sophisticated meal. Manhattan's West Side used to be dot-
ted with small, unpretentious brasseries like Brittany du Soir. It
was staffed with stiff French waiters of the old school who didn't
introduce themselves to you, try to cozy up and flatter you, or tell
you that what you had just ordered was "an excellent choice." They
did not tell you what "Chef" (which has since turned into a proper
noun) had purchased that morning at the farmers' market. They
wore black or white jackets and bow ties. Their hair was oiled and
slick. They minded their manners and performed their duties. You

minded your manners and did the eating. If you had a question, you asked. They answered. Then you got down to the serious business at hand: enjoying a meal of exotic stuff you never ate at home. *Escargots! Artichauts vinaigrette! Quenelles de brochet! Île flottante!* Over dinner, you were also conducting polite, even intense, conversations about life's important issues or crying over romance gone sour. Restaurants were for intimacy, and for intimacy peace and quiet are prerequisites.

Those days are gone forever, like black-and-white television and rotary telephones. In nearly all restaurants, everywhere, it seems, commotion and hysteria have replaced tranquillity.

But not quite everywhere, not yet. Last year, I refreshed my memory of civilized life when, on a trip to Paris, I made a point of eating in highly recommended but not break-the-bank bistros. We sat cheek by jowl with our neighbors, whose food we could see. We could even grab a forkful of it. We could hear their conversations, but only if we listened hard. Why? Everyone was speaking softly. Politesse still existed. I was appeased. But in the States, how many times have you returned from a dinner, having spent a king's ransom, and come down with laryngitis to boot? When did the noise levels in restaurants begin to pose a public health hazard?

I knew I had tapped into some new roar in the zeitgeist more than a decade ago when I went for an early supper with three friends to a now defunct eatery in Dallas. We were the only guests. Music was blaring. I said to the waiter in my gentlest tone, "Would you be so kind as to turn the music down, or off?" He returned with the owner.

"What's the problem?" she inquired.

"The music is so loud we can't hear ourselves talk," I replied imploringly.

"But that's the whole point!" she said.

Things have only grown worse. Recently, I went with a worldly foodie friend to a fancy San Francisco restaurant. We might as well have been at an SMU football game. My dining companion was in heaven; I was at least in purgatory. For our decent but costly meal in a beautiful room, we suffered at the hands of an unctuous waiter who practically sat on our laps, and under deafening noise caused by high ceilings, sound-amplifying tile, loud music, and people screaming. I expressed my discomfort. "It's fun! Dinner as theater!" my friend helpfully explained.

If I want theater, I buy a ticket and go to a theater to see a play. I don't want to witness, let alone participate in, the soap opera on all sides of me, any more than I want to eat architecturally sculpted vertical food. Let's hear it for calm, and relative silence, and a nice plate of things laid out horizontally.

Am I too much an old-fashioned, kvetching purist? I hope not. I am a mild-mannered college professor with excellent hearing and simple tastes. I want good food, pleasant surroundings, and tranquillity. I don't want to walk onto the set of *Sex and the City*. Quiet is a diminishing resource, like water, clean air, and petroleum. Unlike oil, however, there's no reason we cannot regain more of it.

Where does the noise come from? It has three sources, but these make for a kind of chicken-and-egg dilemma. Who knows which came first? Restaurants like to pump up the noise and the music in order to turn tables more quickly, and also to make people think they're dining where the action is. Being where the action is naturally appeals to the young and the hip. So restaurants deliberately use sound-enhancing equipment rather than sound-deadening materials. That's for starters. It doesn't matter whether ceilings are high or low. And, to continue with causes of the din, they turn on the music to fortissimo. Finally, people must scream. When one table screams, the next table screams. On it goes.

Young people—who by and large have not been trained in the niceties of polite conversation, in which people talk one at a time, in quiet voices—tend to be threatened by silence. And they become so used to screaming that even in a quiet place they'll start to yell, and then everyone around them will join in. The noise snowballs.

Regardless of ceilings, acoustics, or music, one's neighbors can spoil everything. Think of your favorite little bistro. You can't pick who will sit next to you. At an intimate restaurant one night, the people beside us were so rambunctious that we couldn't speak across a circular table for six. On my way out, I stopped and said, ever so sweetly, to the group of drunken merrymakers: "Do everyone a favor. The next time you're out, if you're going to be loud, please try to make sure that your conversation isn't so boring." Nonplussed, they continued their revels.

Even when the servers and the hosts try to be helpful, they simply cannot understand what "quiet" means. For a recent Sunday brunch, I walked with a friend into what seemed like a sparsely populated local place. We were greeted by both a smiling hostess and the inevitable musical accompaniment washing over us from speakers on all sides. "Is there a corner where there's no music?" I asked gently and hopefully.

"Certainly," said the obliging hostess. She led us to a side room, even emptier than the main one. We sat at a booth. Then I realized that "no music" does not mean "quiet." Above us on the wall were hung three large television screens broadcasting Sunday's football games. With sound. I summoned the waiter and posed a similar question to him. "Could you turn the television sound off, since no one here is watching the games?"

"Not a problem, sir," he helpfully replied.

After ninety seconds or so of silence, the music came back on. Apparently, one had two choices: music or football. No one in the restaurant could imagine that a third choice was possible.

I have a dream. I want a *boîte du quartier*, a neighborhood place where I can go for a good meal and quiet conversation. What to do? Where to go if you don't want over-upholstered plush, or over-miked rush and glitz where the wild things grow? Where you don't have to take out a second mortgage and can still have a conversation about life's persistent mysteries? Everyone can make recommendations, but you're not always safe. One recent night, I went to a Dallas restaurant where nothing has changed in a quarter century—neither the staff, the menu, the decor, nor the best *pommes frites* in town—and where you hear Handel or Vivaldi, not rock. There were three tables of two and one of six. The last, at the far end of the small restaurant, was full not of raucous kids but of hearing-impaired, screaming eighty-somethings having the time of their lives, thinking they were in their own dining room.

I had three choices: to go over and politely tell them to turn it down, to tell the waiter to do so, or to wait and hope they'd get out soon. I chose option number three, and after forty minutes they hobbled out on their canes and left the rest of us to return to our delicious dinners. And then it came to me: for the best, most civilized meal in town, you might as well stay home.

In the quest for public silence, then, restaurants are out. And, for the most part, so are libraries. Gone are the stern, shushing, schoolmarmish figures who held sway with an iron hand in the libraries of my youth. The main reading room at any university library is liable to sound like an extension of a dormitory. Collaboration has become a mainstay for work in industry, commerce, business, and now in the university. Group tables and open plans have replaced individual desks, cubicles, and offices. Space becomes public and shared, not private and individualized. Teams, rather than solitary people holed up and thinking new thoughts, work together to solve problems, create models, and save the world. At my school, "Engaged Learning" is now a mantra used as a selling point when the university tries to "brand" its product. Students are discouraged from merely reading and writing. These seem selfish and self-indulgent as well as economically useless activities. Instead, we encourage our students to get out into the community with the results of their ideas and research. These may be admirable efforts, but none of them has its origin in the silence of a library carrel where a midnight-oil-burning solitary genius wrestles with feelings and intuitions that may blossom forth into unexpected creations. The library is a buzzing beehive of activity. That activity demands chatter, lots of it.

What does this leave you with if you want silence and solitude? Until they became theme parks and mini-malls, museums offered a ticket to privacy. In my earlier chapter "Art," I describe some recent museum experiences. Before the age of the blockbuster, courtesy of the late Thomas Hoving at the Metropolitan Museum, before gift shops and restaurants rather than the art objects on the other side of the turnstile made museums hot destination spots, you could wander in at lunchtime—many museums had free entry—look at a favorite picture or two, and leave refreshed. Art is supposed to soothe the soul, to calm as well as stimulate the mind. How can this happen when you have to ignore not only the bodies of people between you and what's on the wall but also, and more irksome, those people's often loud outdoor voices as well?

If Keats tried today to hear the soft pipes and spiritual ditties he imagined coming from a Grecian urn, he would fail. The conversations of other museumgoers would drown out his private looking and listening. In "Ode on a Grecian Urn," he finds a temporary escape from living company and real sound through a communion with an imagined art object. He does all the talking; until the very end, the urn remains silent. His personification of the vase takes up, significantly, most of the first stanza and the entire final one of his five-stanza poem. In the middle three, he describes and addresses the figures and scenes depicted on the marble, but at start and finish he addresses the art object itself as a form. He humanizes it tellingly as, in turn, a "bride of quietness," a "foster-child of silence and slow time," a "sylvan historian," a silent teller of tales, who can express certain truths "more sweetly than our rhyme." Its silence is the very essence, as well as the opposite, of sound. These paradoxes gently remind us of what silent art can do. In the last stanza, Keats returns to his personifications but in a different, now negative tone: "O Attic shape! Fair attitude!" and "Cold Pastoral!" The urn "tease[s] us out of thought," because it will give up so little of its mysteries. But disappointment and frustration lead to a modest reconciliation as the urn becomes "a friend to man" and speaks its calming companionable consolations—"'Beauty is truth, truth beauty,'—that is all / Ye know on earth, and all ye need to know"—in the poem's famous conclusion.

Whenever I think of art and the warm friendship it offers, I think also of Thoreau: "I never found the companion that was so companionable as solitude." He was not entirely right. The fourth traditional public venues of what I have called tranquillity are religious sites. Many of these are now in the business of hosting guests, like the journalists I mention above, ordinary secular people who want a weekend away from this world. Even without an elaborate effort to house, feed, and entertain the laity, a religious edifice can offer unintended welcome. An empty chapel encourages contemplation and reverence. You come into a great cathedral from the noisy street to refresh body and soul. And people also gather in the company of like-minded believers—a congregation—for organized worship, in which silent prayer sometimes plays a part. Even those of us without strongly devout leanings can sometimes find sustenance in communal religious settings, through artistic performances or the rituals of weddings and funerals. Sometimes we need to test the waters of our own inchoate yearnings for spirituality. One annoying problem with religious services is not just belief and doctrine but language itself and the human speaking voice. I think of more than the worst offenders: the oily televangelists full of passionate intensity and the blow-dried preachers with pressed hair, bad plastic surgery, and permanent tans. Even those with the best intentions are too often full of palaver, platitudes, and piety.

We writers, readers, and wordsmiths of all types can distrust language as much as we venerate it, and often we want no more of it. We move beyond it or lay it aside. Sick of words, we look for their opposite. When I have a hankering for silence-in-company, I go to a Quaker meeting. There is no doctrine; there is no glamour; there is no shouting. A perfect meeting, for me, is one where no one speaks at all, where at hour's end the day's leader simply turns to her right or left, and says "Good morning" to her neighbor, thereby initiating a round of "Good mornings" around the room. The congregating Friends have been instructed in thoughtfulness and the art of gentle persuasion. America's Founding Quaker Father, William Penn, called "true silence . . . the rest of the mind; it is to the spirit what sleep is to the body, nourishment and refreshment." One speaks when moved to do so by the inner light, and one speaks softly, to the point, and tactfully. The Society of Friends prefers calm reflection to soapbox speechifying. Less is more, and quiet trumps volume.

Think, by contrast, of what passes for conversation on television talk shows, where sound bites and screaming pundits have the upper hand over reasoned discourse and considered phrasing. Human speech, our glory, is also our embarrassment and our shame. We all recognize its inadequacies, its potential for evasion and deception, and also for pure tedium. Language without meaning, like Japanese to me in Kyoto, never annoys you as much as talk heard or even overheard when you know what someone is saying, regardless of the volume. Deafness has its occasional advantages. In his final years, my father lived in what they euphemistically call an "independent senior facility." He had all of his wits and marbles until the end. What he did not have was his hearing. Headsets helped at movies and for his television, telephone, and radio needs. Conversation was difficult. At some point, he needed to send his hearing aids in for cleaning and repair, and he knew he would have to live without them for a week. He said that at the communal meals he would not be able to hear what his tablemates were saying.

"Dad," I said helpfully, "you always complain that the people at your table are very boring. You have an easy out. Just wear a little sign announcing that you will not respond to anything they say because you won't be able to hear them. Just smile and eat." He was placated, even inspired by the knowledge that he would be spared a little tedium.

Perhaps writers cherish quiet more than other people, if only because they know what language can and cannot do. I think of Bob Kaufman, the man who coined the word "beatnik" in the 1950s. He preferred reciting his poems to writing them down, and he knew the Beat avant-garde on both coasts—Ginsberg, Ferlinghetti, Corso, and Kerouac. An itinerant life filled with drugs, run-ins with the police, and psychiatric incarcerations made him an emblem of his times. He also preferred anonymity to publication. In 1963, following the assassination of President Kennedy, Kaufman took a vow of silence and did not speak for another twelve years, until the end of the Vietnam War. Then something changed. The vocalizing switch moved from off to on. In 1975, he walked into a coffee shop and recited his poem "All Those Ships That Never Sailed." Speech had returned to him. Or, rather, he returned to speech. He lived until 1986.

His case was extreme, but not unique. I think of Ezra Pound, incarcerated for madness (rather than the charge of treason that would have been the alternative) following his pro-Fascist, anti-Semitic, and anti-American rants during World War II; when released from Washington's St. Elizabeth's Hospital in 1958, he returned to Italy for the rest of his life. Having talked so much at earlier stages—out of hatred, vitriol, madness, sheer manic exuberance—Pound then retreated. He spoke seldom. I cherish a picture of him and Marianne Moore, two founders of modernist poetics, meeting on a stairway at the New York Public Library in the last year or so of their lives. "Oh, Ezra," said Miss Moore. "Oh, Marianne," said Pound. That sufficed.

Although language fatigues as well as stimulates, you can often move gracefully beyond it, in the way two people can finish each other's sentences or know by a glance what their partner is thinking. Pound and Moore had had enough of words. After a while in any intimate relationship, one can sit in unembarrassed silence with a mate, lover, relative, or close friend, in public as well as in private. It takes time, experience, and patience to reach this stage. It always gave me—and most other adolescents, I imagine—a frisson of sad contempt when I saw a middle-aged couple in a restaurant, mute. They must lack, I thought condescendingly, even stupidly, what John Berryman satirically called "inner resources." They must have no ideas, no new thoughts or perceptions. They seem to prove Thoreau's dismissive remark about "lives of quiet desperation." At the same time, as a vigorously garrulous college student, I watched my grandparents and their friends, well into their seventies, living out the sunset years in a large apartment complex. Parking themselves on a summer evening after dinner in the garden courtyard, they sat, basking quietly in their own company as twilight came on. These were the same people who, a decade or so earlier, had impressed me with their loquacity. With everyone talking all at once, they had made a symphony of speech, in many tones, registers, and volumes. Now I gathered only modest, slow, often half-articulated resignations and recognitions. Bristling with a callow youngster's manic energy and a logomaniac's natural volubility, I pitied them. For the most part, they weren't talking, just sitting, sighing, and acknowledging. I did not realize that they had made their compromise, or better still their peace, with one another and with life, and they had little new to say. I did not know at the time what a different, equally valuable lesson they were teaching me.

In *Another Life*, the story of his family, Michael Korda recounts
the relationship of his father, the art director Vincent Korda, with
Graham Greene:

> My father was famous on three continents for his taciturnity, but
> Graham, normally the most talkative of men, seemed to enjoy
> endless dinners with him, in Antibes, or London, during which
> the two men sat facing each other for hours across a table laden
> with food and drink, never saying a word, apparently quite con-
> tent with each other's company. Once, after a dinner during
> which neither one of them had spoken more than a few words,
> and those about the weather and the food, Graham whispered to
> me as I took him to his waiting taxi, "Your father is the cleverest
> man I know!"

Beckett and Pinter did not invent the pregnant pauses that fill their
plays; they discovered them in ordinary human beings. In a speech,
Pinter once distinguished between a silence in which no word is
spoken and another "when perhaps a torrent of language is being
employed." Everyone can find favorite literary moments in which
silence speaks: Jesus before Caiaphas; Ajax snubbing Odysseus
in Homer's underworld, and Dido doing the same to Aeneas in the
Aeneid; Cordelia articulating the minimal "Nothing" to Lear's
command to match her sisters' fulsome proclamations of filial love;
the list goes on.

Now I know why my taciturn elders, like clever Mr. Korda, had
slowed down and opted for silence. Not because they had limited
intellectual or perceptual resources, but because they did not have
to talk. They had said everything. "Being there together"—as Wallace Stevens memorably put it in his great poem of old age "Final
Soliloquy of the Interior Paramour"—"is enough." Mere presence can take the place of conversation, supplanting noise with

well-earned, all-knowing silence. This senior commitment to quiet is a positive rejoinder to Wittgenstein's famous admonition "Wovon man nicht sprechen kann, darüber muss man schweigen" (Whereof one cannot speak, thereof one must be silent) if only because silence, when elected and not exacted, betokens fulfillment rather than frustration or uncertainty. Instead of being undone by words, you have decided to go without and beyond them.

Does Silence=Death, according to the chilling formula of AIDS activists thirty years ago? In terms of political protest, social repression, and the stifling of dangerous voices, yes. But silence, for Stevens and my grandparents, can embody wisdom. Does a longing for it bring to mind fatigue ("Enough already," I can hear someone say), even a desire for our final end? In *A Time to Keep Silence*, his deeply moving memoir of visits to European monasteries, the late Patrick Leigh Fermor realizes that the silent, obedient Benedictine monks with whom he lived for a month were ready for death at any moment: "The final step would be only a matter of detail."

The final step for almost everyone involves a gradual shutting down of the body and a lessening of all responsiveness. It has long been acknowledged that of all the senses hearing is the last to go. Doctors and other medical personnel know that they should not discuss the situation of a patient—moribund, failing, and perhaps comatose—as though that person cannot hear or understand what they are saying. Often the person can. In his last hospital stay, an uncle of mine gradually lost language, but he revived upon hearing the Gilbert and Sullivan patter songs he had known, loved, and sung as a young man. He mouthed the words as if by rote. They awakened him, and they also awakened something in him that gave pleasure. Next, even when all words had abandoned him, merely hearing the same songs encouraged him to open his eyes. He smiled.

I attended a dying friend last year. He, too, was sinking gradually into the final silence. At first, we conducted conversations. Then, as his mind began to wander and as medications reduced consciousness along with pain, the conversations became more illogical and less linear. A question might stimulate not an answer to it but a metaphorical reply only tangentially related. Things became circular. We spoke in riddles, conundrums, half-truths, and half sentences. It was up to me and others at the bedside to make sense of him, not for him to make sense of or to us. A sentence would start and drift away. Whole articulations gave way to random words. Then whispers. I would press his hand—his eyes being shut—and talk to him as though I were talking with him. Sometimes, his eyes opened and signaled some responsiveness. Sometimes, he squeezed my hand in reciprocity. Finally, I alone spoke. I imagine he heard. I hope that he heard. His silence might have implied his impending death, but it did not mean that he could not understand.

In a secular life, the choice of silence may augur a yearning for ordinary peace and quiet, for death's gentler second self, which we may label rest. Eighty years ago, the literary critic William Empson defined and explored what he labeled "versions of pastoral." Consider Andrew Marvell's paradigmatic poem "The Garden." The poet finds respite, an escape from the external world, via a flight to a *locus amoenus*, the traditional pastoral "pleasing place" of inwardness and silence. The pastoral mode balances equal parts of innocence and experience, simplicity and sophistication. It is what Marvell seeks, and discovers, in the imagined garden:

> Fair Quiet, have I found thee here,
> And Innocence, thy sister dear!
> Mistaken long, I sought you then
> In busy companies of men:
> Your sacred plants, if here below,
> Only among the plants will grow;

> Society is all but rude,
> To this delicious solitude.

The scene implies contrasts: before-and-after in time, and there-and-here in space. Marvell pictures solitude after society; silence after bustle; innocence after worldliness; sweetness rather than rudeness; a replacement of male company (the plural "companies" suggests military troops rather than mere companionship) with a pair of allegorical ladies, Innocence and Quiet. Ordinary secular people can achieve this longed-for condition in moments of vacation or a Sunday rest after six days of work. For Marvell, the Garden is the spot for relaxed, solitary inwardness, for the almost impossible condition of aloneness. Even Adam and Eve didn't have it so good: "Two Paradises 'twere in one / To live in Paradise alone." One is company; two's a crowd.

Students of pastoral all acknowledge, if only tacitly, that the final pastoral condition, the one that meets all the demands for quiet, even total silence, requires the inevitable loss of all consciousness. In his magisterial *The Oaten Flute*, Renato Poggioli labeled this "the pastoral of death." In 1815, Wordsworth, experiencing an exciting, though unspecified, gust of passion ("Surprised by joy—impatient as the Wind"), turns, or so he thinks, to his daughter Catherine, whose death he has momentarily forgotten. She is no longer available: "I turned to share the transport—Oh! with whom / But Thee, deep buried in the silent tomb, / That spot which no vicissitude can find?" Those of us who seek silence, or at least quiet, will have to stay on the qui vive, seeking it out when and where we can, balancing our civic, social, and personal obligations to others with our selfish need to withdraw into our own happiness (to paraphrase Marvell) slowly. The final silence will come all too soon, and only in the tomb. Until then, we'll remain satisfied with its gentler, more modest, enabling, and ennobling surrogates.

Sometimes we give in to silence, but often we come back for

one last exchange. Some people leave without saying goodbye. Others say goodbye without actually leaving. I shall allow Walt Whitman, master of sociable tenderness as well as braggadocio, to have the final word. He knew about farewells and endings as well as anyone; he offers the most poignant literary defense of talkativeness before the final silence:

> After the supper and talk—after the day is done,
> As a friend from friends his final withdrawal prolonging,
> Good-bye and Good-bye with emotional lips repeating,
> (So hard for his hand to release those hands—no more will
>   they meet,
> No more for communion of sorrow and joy, of old and
>   young,
> A far-stretching journey awaits him, to return no more,)
> Shunning, postponing severance—seeking to ward off the
>   last word ever so little,
> E'en at the exit-door turning—charges superfluous calling
>   back—e'en as he descends the steps,
> Something to eke out a minute additional—shadows of
>   nightfall deepening,
> Farewells, messages lessening—dimmer the forthgoer's
>   visage and form,
> Soon to be lost for aye in the darkness—loth, O so loth to
>   depart!
> Garrulous to the very last.

This is the Whitman not of the "barbaric yawp" but of the resigned whisper. His poem's present participles and gerunds pile up on top of one another, their sounds doubling and redoubling ("final withdrawal prolonging," "emotional lips repeating," "far-stretching," "shunning, postponing," "seeking," "turning," "calling," "deepening," "lessening"). The amassing of vocal and physical gestures comes to a halt before we even realize that this is a nonsentence, or rather a sentence with no simple verb. Everything is deferred or withheld, a conversation constantly in medias res, stretching through time as the departing comrade, "loth to depart," is equally loath to enter into silence, which for him would indeed be death. Talk is our essence. Whitman brings sight and sound together: soon to be lost in the darkness means soon to be lost in silence, too. As at the end of Revelation, sound accompanies the parting shot: here, not the trumpet's last call, but the poet's ongoing, gently garrulous babble.

ACKNOWLEDGMENTS

Martha Kaplan and Jonathan Galassi, once and present agent and editor, make writing and publishing a pleasure. I owe them more than polite recognition. At FSG, Jo Stewart, Susan Goldfarb, and Lottchen Shivers helped my book see the light of day, as did the copy editor, Ingrid Sterner.

Some of the material in this book has appeared in abbreviated form elsewhere. I have revised and expanded my original thoughts. I offer my thanks to the editors who worked with me at earlier stages: Sudip Bose and Robert Wilson (*The American Scholar*); Ben Downing and Herbert Leibowitz (*Parnassus*); Wade Lambert (*The Wall Street Journal*); J. D. McClatchy (*The Yale Review*); Mark Oppenheimer (*New Haven Review*); and Paula Marantz Cohen and Diane Pizzuto (*The Smart Set*).

When I was in the process of composing and arranging this book's contents, I began to give serious thought as well to its title. Several friends received one early possibility, "Senior Happiness," with disapproval or disdain. One of them said jokingly, "Well, at least you won't call it *Senior Moments*." A light came on. I owe a debt of gratitude to this person for the illumination, but I must pay the debt anonymously. I cannot for the life of me remember who gave me this delicious and unexpected suggestion.